# American Secondary Education

## The Conant Influence

A Look at Conant's Recommendations
for Senior and Junior High Schools

A. Harry Passow

[redacted]

National Association of Secondary School Principals
Reston, Virginia

*About the Author:* A. Harry Passow is the Jacob H. Schiff Professor of Education and Director, Division of Educational Institutions and Programs, Teachers College, Columbia University, New York, N.Y.

ISBN 0-88210-086-6


National Association of Secondary School Principals
1904 Association Drive
Reston, Virginia 22091

# Contents

JAMES BRYANT CONANT, born in Boston, Mass., on March 26, 1893, earned both his A.B. (1913) and Ph.D. (1916) at Harvard. He served as Professor of Chemistry at Harvard from 1919 to 1933, when he became President, a position he held for 20 years. In 1953, Conant served as the High Commissioner for Germany and in 1955 became the first Ambassador to West Germany, a position he held until 1957. On returning to the United States, he began a number of studies of American education, supported to a large extent through grants from the Carnegie Corporation of New York.

Conant's early publications included a high school chemistry textbook as well as other textbooks on organic chemistry. A renowned chemist, Conant was involved in the Manhattan Project from which the first atomic bomb was developed. Until his retirement from active professional life, Conant authored numerous books on education and was involved in studies of various aspects of American education. It is his involvement with American education—particularly secondary education—that is the focus of this monograph.

# Foreword

Twenty years ago James Bryant Conant began a study that resulted in the publication of *The American High School Today: A First Report to Interested Citizens.* In typical Conant style he wrote and spoke simply but vigorously on strengthening the nation's secondary schools. Ten years later, as chairman of NASSP's Committee on the Study of the American Secondary School, he presented *The Comprehensive High School*, which constituted a second major report to interested citizens. In both studies he avoided hearsay evidence and the cacophonous drumbeat of the critics, and went directly to the schools for first-hand observations. As was to be expected, some of his recommendations proved to be controversial but all were on the target with the overriding objective to improve the quality of our schools.

This year marked the tenth and twentieth anniversaries of these scholarly works and it seemed fitting that NASSP reassess the impact of the Conant decades. A distinguished colleague, A. Harry Passow of Columbia University, was chosen to undertake the project. Both Dr. Passow and your Executive Director were privileged to know and work with James Bryant Conant which gave the resulting monograph additional color.

There can be no question as to Dr. Conant's monumental contributions or his place in history. He truly is one of the giants of American education. Every facet of our junior and senior high school programs was investigated and carefully weighed, and the ingredient of specificity added to each and every one of his recommendations for improvement. During the 1977 anniversary year his findings and suggestions are still worthy of review by layman and professional alike. His championing the cause of secondary education makes him unique in this century and our schools are better for his having passed this way. All of us remain in his debt.

Owen B. Kiernan
*Executive Director*, NASSP

# Introduction

ON MARCH 1, 1957, HAVING JUST returned from an assignment as the high commissioner and then the ambassador to the Federal Republic of West Germany, James Bryant Conant met with the president of the Carnegie Corporation of New York, John W. Gardner, and five other persons[1] to discuss a proposal for a study of the American high school which Conant had submitted to Gardner several months earlier.[2] By the end of the month, the nature and design of the study was broadened, the Carnegie Corporation funded the study, and James Bryant Conant was launched on what was to become a series of studies of American education which were to occupy the remainder of his active professional life.

In his memoirs, Conant wrote:

> If someone had told me when I was a chemist that in my old age I would devote a considerable amount of time and energy to examining the public high schools of the United States, I should have branded him as demented. I had no interest in secondary education and never expected to develop any. Even if a similar prophecy had been made in the first year or two of my Harvard presidency, I should have thought the prediction far from the mark. Only after Professor Spaulding had opened my eyes to some of the problems in American secondary education would I have agreed that I might someday devote all my time to matters connected with schools rather than colleges and universities.[3]

While on home leave in early 1956, Conant met with Gardner and discussed Conant's future after he retired from diplomatic work. Gardner indicated that the Carnegie Corporation would look favorably on a proposal by Conant to do something related to education.

---

1. James Perkins, vice president of Carnegie Corporation; William Carr, executive secretary of the National Education Association; Francis Keppel, dean of Harvard University Graduate School of Education; Henry Chauncey, president of the Educational Testing Service; and John H. Fischer, superintendent of the Baltimore Public Schools.
2. J. B. Conant, *My Several Lives: Memoirs of a Social Inventor*, New York: Harper and Row, 1970, p. 618.
3. *Ibid.*, p. 613.

Within six months, having declined an invitation to serve as the U.S. Ambassador to India, Conant was thinking about leaving the diplomatic field and re-entering education. While in New York during Christmas 1956, Conant met with Gardner and set forth his ideas for a project. A memorandum he dictated began as follows:

> What is proposed is a study of the education of the talented youth of a community in an American comprehensive high school (senior and junior high schools). The study would be conducted by me personally with the assistance of three or four collaborators. I would propose to be responsible for the findings and the conclusions. Any recommendations would be put forward under my own name and on my own responsibility. To be useful the project must be completed, including publication, in two years. The proposed date for starting the work would be October 1, 1957.[4]

Conant's original memorandum proposed a study of provisions for the talented youth in high schools in four states—Pennsylvania, New Jersey, New York, and Connecticut. However, the group which met with Conant at the Carnegie Corporation on March 1, urged him to broaden his geographic coverage, to deal with the comprehensive high school as a whole, to do the on-site visitation of schools himself, and to secure a staff of educators who could assist with school visits and data collection.

Thus, Conant's study had been planned and was well underway several months before the advent of Sputnik in October 1957. The study was clearly not undertaken in response to the waves of criticism of America's secondary schools. Beginning in the mid-1930s and continuing into the post-World War II period, high schools came under ever sharper attacks from a variety of sources. Writing about these years in a chapter titled, "The Crisis in Popular Education," Cremin observed:

> A spate of books, articles, pamphlets, radio programs, and television panels burst upon the pedagogical scene, airing every ailment of the schools, real and imaginary. One result was the most vigorous, searching, and fundamental attack on progressive education since the beginning of the movement.[5]

---

4. *Ibid.*, p. 617.
5. L. A. Cremin, *The Transformation of the School*, New York: Alfred Knopf, 1961, p. 339.

## A Long Concern with American Education

A RENOWNED CHEMIST WHOSE textbooks were standard works in the field, president of Harvard University, academic educator, participant in the *Manhattan Project* (development of atomic bomb), international statesman and diplomat, Conant had long been interested in American education. In fact, the antecedents for much of what he was to say in his post-1957 reports can be found in his earlier writings. Conant has recounted how he spent time with German educators while he was in Bonn as high commissioner and had translated parts of his book, *Education in a Divided World,* into German.

Conant felt, however, that his "exposition of American education and its goals suffered from at least one defect. My knowledge of American schools was all second-hand."[6] It was from this reflection that he decided that when his tour of duty as ambassador was finished, he would try to find some excuse for visiting American schools—at least to the extent that he had visited Australian and New Zealand schools earlier. Such visits, he observed, would serve the purpose of at least satisfying his own curiosity about the degree of exactness concerning what he had been telling the Germans about American schools.

Conant had joined the Educational Policies Commission in 1941, a move which he describes as having "crucial significance" for him in broadening his educational concerns: "I learned from the fellow members of the Commission about the realities of public education and the goals of those who were trying to develop schools which would provide for *all* American youth."[7] During one of the first meetings in which Conant participated in January 1942, the Educational Policies Commission drafted a report titled, *A War Policy for American Schools*. Conant drew on his knowledge of the English educational system to make suggestions for the report.

In 1945, Conant delivered the Julius and Rosa Sachs Memorial Lectures at Teachers College, Columbia University. His three lectures were titled: "The Structure of American Society," "General Education for American Society," and "Education Beyond High School." In these lectures he directed attention to the interaction

6. Conant, *My Several Lives*, p. 614.
7. *Ibid.*, p. 613.

between the nation's social structure and its formal education process. His basic thesis, one which he thought clearly expressed his educational and social philosophy, he stated as follows:

> One of the highly significant ideals of the American nation has been equality of opportunity. This ideal implies on the one hand a relatively fluid social structure changing from generation to generation, and on the other mutual respect between different vocational and economic groups; in short, a minimum of emphasis on class distinctions. It is of the utmost significance for our future that belief in this ideal be strengthened and that we move each year nearer to its realization in our practice. In our modern industrialized society, national educational policy largely determines the future of our social structure. In the last fifty years educational forces have been at work which have tended to stratify the American nation. On the other hand, a vast instrument of American democracy has been created by the extension of universal education to the high school stage. If we so desire, this instrument can restore a high degree of fluidity to our social and economic life; we can make available for the national welfare reservoirs of potential talent now untapped. Furthermore, education can inculcate the social and political ideals necessary for the development of a free and harmonious people operating an economic system based on private ownership and the profit motive but committed to the ideals of social justice. The nearer we approach through education to our avowed goal of equality of opportunity (which, however, admittedly can never be reached) and the better our schools teach and practice the basic tenets of American democracy, the more chance there is for personal liberty as we know it to continue in these United States.[8]

This basic thesis—an expression of fundamental belief in democracy and equality of educational opportunity—is one that permeates Conant's writings. In these lectures, Conant commented that he had "borrowed freely" from the Educational Policies Commission publication, *Education for All American Youth,* and the Harvard Committee report, *General Education in a Free Society,* and that he had been much impressed by the Warner, Havighurst, and Loeb publication, *Who Shall Be Educated?*[9]

8. J. B. Conant, "Public Education and the Structure of American Education," *Teachers College Record,* December 1945, pp. 145-194.
9. Educational Policies Commission, *Education for All American Youth* (Washington, D.C.: National Education Association, 1944). Harvard Committee on General Education, *General Education in a Free Society* (Cambridge: Harvard University Press, 1945). W. L. Warner, R. J. Havighurst, and M. B. Loeb, *Who Shall Be Educated?* (New York: Harper and Brothers, 1944).

Conant argued that education, as "perhaps the most important process in determining the future of our country," required a larger portion of our national income and that federal aid to education—money appropriated by Congress but spent by the states and localities without restriction—was the only way to provide such financial resources.

In Conant's view, both the Educational Policies Commission and the Harvard Committee on General Education reports dealt with how the curriculum of the high school should provide for both general and vocational education, and were, in reality, not too far apart. The differences, he commented, were in the way subjects were put together—"one according to a pattern which corresponds to the rational method of handling areas of knowledge traditional in our universities, the other in terms of stimulating the interests of those students who have no natural bent for scholarly work."[10] The reports set forth different reasons for a common core of general education and provide different rationales for including certain subjects in a course of common learnings.

Conant was already interested in the academically talented and urged university professors to avoid judging high schools in terms of their success or failure in the education of specially gifted youth. Rather, he proposed that high school educators agree:

> (a) to provide a greater motivation among many groups to evolve a higher degree of intellectual curiosity; (b) to explore more sympathetically the ways and means of discovering special talent at an early age; and (c) to provide better formal instruction for those of high scholastic aptitude—all this to be accomplished without a segregation which might turn the boys and girls in question into either prigs or academic snobs.[11]

Conant's first book on education, *Education in a Divided World*, although based on his Sachs Lectures, bore, as he put it, "little resemblance to those lectures." In his preface, Conant pointed to a need to appeal to citizens to interest themselves in the American system of public education. Experience over the years had convinced Conant that hostility to the public schools was widespread. He wrote:

> This hostility was based on ignorance of the present practices in

10. Conant, "Public Education and the Structure of American Education," p. 176.
11. *Ibid.*, p. 178.

> schools and above all of the nature of the task they had been called to undertake. It was to be found as strongly among ardent supporters of the New Deal as among the most conservative opponents of the Roosevelt administration....With this attitude of many laymen in mind, I decided to alter the objective of my examination of public education and the structure of American society so as to make it the basis for a frank plea to the citizens of this republic to stop, look, and see their schools in operation, and consider the relation of the teachers' work to the future of this nation.[12]

In this book, Conant argued for strengthening our public schools, and just as he was to do with his first report on comprehensive high school, he wrote to "interested citizens":

> The free tax-supported schools are the sinews of our society: they are the product of our unique ideals and the vehicle by which the American concept of democracy may be transmitted to our future citizens. The strength of this republic is therefore intimately connected with the success or failure of our system of public education.[13]

Conant provided additional details of his notion of general education with a discussion of the curriculum for the humanities, the study of man, and the natural sciences. In a chapter on "Education for a Career," Conant again focused primarily on the secondary school curriculum for the talented youth. He offered three criteria to judge the effectiveness of secondary schools for the gifted boy: (1) "the intellecutal interests of the student must be keenly stimulated during the entire last four years of his school work;" (2) "the inculcation of a belief in the relevance of formal study and 'book learning' to the problems of the day;" and (3) acquisition of work habits, "the ability to knuckle down and do a hard intellectual job."

A concern with vocational education—what is later expressed by Conant in terms of the "acquisition of marketable skills"—was set forth and Conant argued for such training to take place in a comprehensive high school: "Such differentiation as is required will be within one school and should be so arranged as to create as little social distinction as possible."[14]

Conant concluded *Education in a Divided World* with a plea for citizen involvement and support for the public schools:

---

12. J. B. Conant, *Education in a Divided World* (Cambridge: Harvard University Press, 1947), p. viii.
13. *Ibid.*, p. 1.
14. *Ibid.*, p. 152.

> Our unique contribution is not in abstract thought nor in art nor poetry. It is rather in a demonstration that a certain type of society long dreamed of by idealists can be closely approached in reality—a free society in which the hopes and aspirations of a larger fraction of the members find enduring satisfaction through outlets once reserved for only a small minority of mankind. To bring us still closer to this reality should be the aim of educators in the United States. To assist them in this undertaking, all thoughtful citizens might well rally to the support of public education. For only by their labors can this vast instrument of democracy be made responsive to the needs of a free nation in a divided world.[15]

In his second book about education, *Education and Liberty,* Conant reported on a study of secondary education in Australia and New Zealand. This book was based on three Page-Barbour Lectures he had delivered at the University of Virginia. Conant compared British and American secondary education (Australia and New Zealand having developed educational traditions stemming from England and Scotland) and examined the "American invention," the four-year liberal arts college and its influences on the high school. In the final chapter (third lecture), Conant discussed the unique aspects of the comprehensive high school and considered the criticisms then being leveled at it.

In his memoirs, Conant observed that the last pages of this book might well have been titled, "A Defense of the Comprehensive High School." In the preface, he observed:

> As everyone is well aware, there is today an increased critical discussion of the role of the high schools in our American democracy. For many decades their aims and their methods have been subject to constant scrutiny, not only by professionals, but also by parents and citizens. This had been an important feature of their development. The local communities in this country have shaped their schools far more than in any other nation. That this is so is one of the significant aspects of our American pattern of tax-supported education. Through the device of community responsibility we have avoided to a larger degree the danger of a state-imposed uniformity. Our multitude of local school boards provide a great diversity while each one aims at being a center for developing a spirit of democratic cooperation.[16]

15. *Ibid.*, p. 235.
16. J. B. Conant, *Education and Liberty: The Role of Schools in a Modern Democracy* (Cambridge: Harvard University Press, 1963), p. xi.

The pattern of public education which had evolved provided, in Conant's view, "a great engine of democracy which has served this nation of many creeds." Without the public schools, Conant doubted whether such a culturally diverse nation could have found "a common basis of understanding." The work of the public schools was hardly complete and many schools fell far short of the ideal. The problem he posed—"Shall we improve the schools or change the pattern?"

Clearly, Conant's biases were in favor of improvement rather than change—a very firm position he was to take again a half dozen years later. As Conant saw it, the doctrine of equality about which De Tocqueville had written a century earlier had come to mean equality of opportunity for the young rather than parity of status for all adults. The expansion of secondary education, in Conant's view, had created a new vehicle for nurturing the American concept of democracy.

Assuming that the number of adolescents would increase by some 50 percent within a few years, Conant set forth 10 suggestions for the future of colleges and secondary schools, including four directed toward secondary schools:

- We continue the expansion of our junior and senior high schools to meet the new bulge in the enrollments, but in so doing, recognize the need for remaking the curriculum in many schools.

- We adhere to the principle of a comprehensive high school with a common core of studies and differentiated special programs, but in so doing we make far more effort to identify the gifted youth and give him or her more rigorous academic training in languages and mathematics.

- We explore the success of some high schools in recent years with "work experience programs" and expand these programs, including particularly the thirteenth and fourteenth grades (the two-year college).

- We continue to experiment with general education at every level for the future manual worker, the future salesman or executive, and the most highly specialized university graduate.[17]

17. *Ibid.*, p. 57-58.

Noting little of a novel nature in his own suggestions, Conant emphasized that what he was advocating was simply a continuing drive for general education which he viewed as a uniquely American characteristic. The suggestions reflected "a belief in the value for *all* American youth of a study of history, the elements of political science, economics, sociology, and geography, some illustrations of the methods of the natural sciences, together with a study of literature and the arts conducted with due regard for developing emotional maturation and wisdom."[18]

Here once again, Conant stressed a common, general education for *all* youth and detailed the "subjects" which he believed constituted such a general education. Moreover, Conant was convinced that the place for such a general education was a comprehensive high school:

> My proposals are also based on my conviction that as far as possible the public schools in the United States should be schools where the youth of very different backgrounds and outlooks share a common experience, where the extracurricular activities and at least a common core of studies including English should cut across vocational interests and cover a wide range of scholastic aptitudes.[19]

Conant had serious reservations about separating youth on the basis of academic ability and vocational aspirations since such practice failed "to provide a basis for the growth of mutual understanding between different cultural, religious, and occupational groups."[20] The elementary schools and the high schools in small cities and towns were providing this unifying function without which, Conant believed, America could not have developed its remarkable coherence despite its cultural diversity and great size. As he put it: "The concept of education as a social process, combined with a belief in the American idea of democracy and a concern with national unity, lead to the conclusion that a first-rate comprehensive high school is the ideal."[21]

Conant freely acknowledged that his concept of the comprehensive high school did not exist in many localities and fell far short of the ideal in many more. This was especially true in the southern states where *de jure* segregated schools still existed and in larger

18. *Ibid.*, p. 59.
19. *Ibid.*
20. *Ibid.*, p. 62.
21. *Ibid.*

cities where high schools served neighborhoods that were separated on the basis of socioeconomic, racial, or ethnic lines. Where such problems existed, he felt, they did not indicate the failure of the concept of the comprehensive high school but instead pointed "to the need for planning educational development with an eye to sociology as well as pedagogy."

It was not that the comprehensive high schools did not have shortcomings in Conant's view. He discussed and considered some of these, including the adequacy of education for the gifted, the limitations of the application of the doctrine of equality of opportunity, and the availability of work-experience programs and part-time education.

Conant also examined the controversy and competition between public and private (including parochial) schools, arguing that growth of private schools constituted a danger to the public schools in a community. His remarks appeared to be aimed at those critics of public education who were using such criticisms to enhance the cause of private education.

Conant concluded his Page-Barbour Lectures with the observation that considerable progress had been made in the preceding 25 years in providing for all American youth—this despite many inadequacies in high schools and the still undeveloped nature of the two-year community colleges. He urged educators to "endeavor to combine the British concern for training the 'natural aristocracy of talents' with the American insistence on general education for *all* future citizens."[22]

In February 1953, Conant became the high commissioner to the Federal Republic of Germany. In a lecture delivered in Boston sometime earlier, Conant had argued against financing private (and parochial) schools with public tax money—a position which he expanded and clarified in *Education and Liberty*.

At the Senate hearings, his views on financing private schools were questioned by opponents to his confirmation as high commissioner. He was asked, for example, whether he felt the German system of confessional schools was incompatible with democracy. During his service as high commissioner and later ambassador, Conant had occasional contact with German educators and educational planners. This period was also marked by an appearance at a

22. *Ibid.*, p. 87.

hearing chaired by Senator Joseph McCarthy investigating the alleged presence of some "30,000 publications by Communist authors on information shelves" in West Germany. His account of these experiences with McCarthy provides additional insights into Conant's character and his values.[23]

## A Study of the American High School

THE AMERICAN HIGH SCHOOL–the 140-page report of his study of the comprehensive high school—was clearly a product of the mind of James Bryant Conant. In his memorandum to John Gardner in December 1956, setting forth his ideas about the study, Conant indicated that the study would be conducted by him personally, with the assistance of three or four collaborators, and that he himself would be responsible for the findings, the conclusions, and the recommendations. Of the 103 schools in 26 states which were visited, Conant himself visited at least 55 high schools. (The report gives "a total of fifty-five in 18 of the more populous states" and in his memoirs he mentions visiting "no less than fifty-nine high schools, most of which had been recommended as among the best in the United States.") The field work was done during the academic year 1957-58.

Aside from visits to schools, Conant met with a variety of lay and professional individuals and groups to test out his ideas, to have them criticized, and to hear new suggestions. The "Acknowledgement" in the front of the published report[24] was dated November 10, 1958. He had kept to the schedule he had drawn up at the outset.

The report's 21 recommendations as well as analytic material on the characteristics of American education and the comprehensive high school represented ideas that Conant had thought about for a long time, as reflected in his writings beginning with the three Sachs

23. Conant, *My Several Lives*, pp. 561-79.
24. J. B. Conant, *The American High School Today: A First Report to Interested Citizens* (New York: McGraw-Hill, 1959).

Memorial Lectures he had delivered at Teachers College, Columbia University, in 1945.

In the Foreword to the book, John W. Gardner wrote:

> It would be hard to find anyone better equipped to make such a study at this moment in our history. At the summit of a career of distinguished service to education and to the nation, Mr. Conant's capacity to command public confidence is great and well deserved. His devotion to rigorous intellectual training and his dedication to the social and political principles which animate this nation are both vitally important qualifications for the job.[25]

The comprehensive high school, Gardner observed, is a "peculiarly American phenomenon."

> It is called comprehensive because it offers, under one administration and under one roof (or series of roofs), secondary education for almost all the high school age children of one town or neighborhood. It is responsible for educating the boy who will be an atomic scientist and the girl who will marry at eighteen; the prospective captain of a ship and the future captain of industry. It is responsible for educating the bright and the not so bright children with different vocational and professional ambitions and with various motivations. It is responsible, in sum, for providing good and appropriate education, both academic and vocational, for all young people within a democratic environment which the American people believe serves the principles they cherish.[26]

Gardner's description of the comprehensive high school was essentially what Conant had been using over the years. And, while there were those who would and did argue with this idealized notion of the American comprehensive high school, it was in fact the ideal that guided Conant's study.

Conant's terse description of the characteristics of American education in his opening section traced the evolution of America's public schools, colleges, and universities by comparing and contrasting American and European education from an historical perspective, as he had done earlier. He concluded, "As a consequence of the changes in universities and colleges in the nineteenth century and the alteration of the employment situation since World War I, the American public high school has become an institution which

25. *Ibid.*, p. ix.
26. *Ibid.*, pp. ix-x.

has no counterpart in any other country."[27] There have been other interpretations of the shaping of the American high school but Conant's very brief summary of the characteristics of American public education was consistent with his earlier analyses.

Conant viewed the doctrine of local responsibility and community independence as part of America's pioneer history and deliberately directed his report to interested citizens—specifically to school board members. Gardner recommended the report not for those "interested in venting their prejudices or in beating one another about the ears with slogans and battle cries" but rather for those who would roll up their sleeves and ask, "Precisely what can we do tomorrow morning to improve our schools?"[28] Conant later wrote in his memoirs:

> The timing was perfect. A wave of public criticism of the high schools which had started after Sputnik had reached its crest. School board members all over the country were anxious for our specific answers to such questions as: "How should we organize our schools?"; "What should the high schools teach?" We supplied the answers boldly and categorically in twenty-one specific recommendations.[29]

Recognizing that there are three- and four-year high schools, Conant preferred to think in terms of a four-year scheme insofar as program development was concerned and his recommendations deal with grades nine through 12. He acknowledged the existence of specialized high schools—some which offer programs for a special group of students (e.g., academic or college preparatory) and others which provide vocational programs. He also recognized that the comprehensiveness of some high schools was limited not by the availability of specialized schools, but rather by a lack of interest in the community in certain types of programs which develop special skills immediately useful upon graduation.

Conant focused his study on what he described as schools with "a high degree of comprehensiveness," schools which tended to exhibit the following characteristics:

- They provided a variety of vocational programs since more than half the students terminated full-time study upon graduation from high school.

---

27. *Ibid.*, p. 7.
28. *Ibid.*, pp. xi-xii.
29. Conant, *My Several Lives*, p. 621.

- They provided special programs for those who have high academic ability.
- They had, as a prime objective, nurturing a democratic school spirit and fostering understanding between students with different vocational goals and intellectual abilities.
- They had graduating classes of at least 100 students.
- They were located in smaller cities and towns (populations between 10,000 and 100,000) since large cities often provided vocational and/or specialized high schools and surburban communities tended not to have strong vocational programs.

The specific question that Conant sought to answer with his study was: "Can a school at one and the same time provide a good general education for *all* the pupils as future citizens of a democracy, provide elective programs for the majority to develop useful skills, and educate adequately those with a talent for handling advanced academic subjects—particularly foreign languages and mathematics?"[30]

The answer to this question, Conant observed, had considerable significance for the future of American secondary education. A radical change in the structure of American secondary education would be needed if the answer were clearly negative. If the answer were an affirmative one, then no radical alteration would be needed in the basic pattern of American education. (At this time, Admiral Rickover was one of the most vocal spokespersons questioning the very existence of the comprehensive high schools as the prototype institution for serving the educational needs of America's youth.)

Conant cautioned readers that his was *not* an evaluative study of the comprehensive high school since there were too many differences among the 21,000 public high schools. Rather, Conant sought the answer to determine whether there were schools which did fulfill the objectives of a comprehensive high school so that such schools could serve as models or patterns.

The 103 schools involved in Conant's study were not selected by any scientific sampling procedures. Conant asked various sources for the names of comprehensive high schools not located in metropolitan areas, "which had the reputation of doing a good job in providing education for students with a wide range of vocational inter-

30. *Ibid.*, p. 15.

ests and abilities," which had a college-going population of less than half the graduating class, and which had a normal range of academic ability (median I.Q. 100-105). From a dozen or so nominations in each state Conant and his staff selected not more than three or four.

After a few initial visits to schools, a checklist was developed to assist Conant and his colleagues in judging the comprehensiveness of the high schools observed. The list was as follows:

A. Adequacy of general education for all as judged by:
   1. Offerings in English and American literature and composition
   2. Social studies, including American history
   3. Ability grouping in required courses

B. Adequacy of nonacademic elective program as judged by:
   4. The vocational programs for boys and commercial programs for girls
   5. Opportunities for supervised work experience
   6. Special provisions for very slow readers

C. Special arrangement for the academically talented students:
   7. Special provisions for challenging the highly gifted
   8. Special instruction in developing reading skills
   9. Summer sessions from which able students may profit
   10. Individualized programs (absence of tracks or rigid programs)
   11. School day organized into seven or more instructional periods

D. Other features:
   12. Adequacy of the guidance service
   13. Student morale
   14. Well-organized homerooms
   15. The success of the school in promoting an understanding between students with widely different academic abilities and vocational goals (effective social interaction among students).[31]

In addition to judging the schools on the above 15 points, Conant talked with teachers of mathematics, science, and foreign languages, visited their classes, and met with students to ascertain the adequacy of offerings in these subject areas and the effectiveness of the

---

31. *Ibid.*, pp. 19-20.

teaching. He explored provisions for the academically talented with teachers and guidance counselors. And, he had principals of 22 schools complete what he called an "academic inventory"—an inventory summarizing the programs of the twelfth grade academically talented students, the top 15 percent in a school with a normal range of intellectual ability.

Conant decided that his question could be answered in the affirmative. He wrote: *"I found eight schools which, in my judgment, were satisfactorily fulfilling the three main objectives of a comprehensive high school."*[32]

These schools were offering adequate instruction as part of the general education for all in English and social studies; were providing significant nonacademic programs which a substantial number of students were electing to take; and a majority of the academically talented boys (not so for the academically talented girls) were studying at least seven years of mathematics and science and seven years of social studies and English.

Conant found the situation with respect to foreign languages in these schools less satisfactory. Except for the academically talented girls in five of the eight schools, the academically talented were not studying a foreign language for three years.

Conant made 21 "specific recommendations addressed to school board members and school administrators" which, he felt, taken together provided an outline of "the important characteristics of a satisfactory high school which is widely comprehensive."[33] Describing his recommendations as "conservative" and "necessarily presented in dogmatic form," Conant stressed the importance of innovation and experimentation and hoped that his recommendations would not be seen as his favoring the freezing of either the development of the curriculum or the organization of a high school. He pointed out that he could readily draw up a long list of urgent problems in secondary education which could only be solved by schools testing and evaluating new ideas and did, in fact, provide some examples of "a new spirit of examination of the high school curriculum." Conant observed:

> Ten or even five years from now, at least some of my recommendations may need serious revision because of what has been demonstrated as successful practice. In short, there is no inconsistency

32. *Ibid.*, p. 22.
33. *Ibid.*, p. 41.

between adapting the best from what has been well tried and tested and having an open mind about the outcome of experiments newly planned or underway.[34]

Conant's first recommendation focused on the counseling system, urging articulation between the various levels (i.e., elementary, junior high, and senior high) and suggesting that there be a full-time counselor or guidance officer for every 250-300 students. Conant made specific suggestions as to how these counselors were to function, especially with respect to the elective programs that develop marketable skills and the guidance of the more able students and the slow readers.

A second recommendation suggested that every student be provided an individualized program with classifications according to tracks or labeled programs (e.g., "college preparatory" or "vocational") eliminated. There was to be a required program for all and certain minimum elective program requirements for the academically talented and those who needed to develop marketable skills, but Conant urged considerable flexibility and guidance service support.

Conant was very specific on what should be a required program for all students and provided considerable detail concerning what he considered "general education." For graduation, all students would be required to take:

> . . .four years of English, three or four years of social studies—including two years of history (one of which should be American history) and a senior course in American problems or American government—one year of mathematics in the ninth grade (algebra or general mathematics), and at least one year of science in the ninth or tenth grade, which might well be biology or general physical science.[35]

Conant defined a "year" as a course meeting five periods a week for an academic year or an equivalent amount of time. The general education academic program (involving nine or 10 courses) constituted more than half the students' time; the other seven or more courses (not including physical education) were to be chosen from electives. Conant urged that all students include art and music in these elective programs and that the other electives be chosen from

34. *Ibid.*, pp. 43-44.
35. *Ibid.*, p. 47.

a particular course sequence, leading either to the development of a marketable skill or academic skills. He proposed that clear standards be set for passing and failing courses and that these high standards be maintained.

Conant proposed that half the total time (four years) devoted to English should involve the student in English composition with an average of one theme a week required. So that English teachers could read and correct these themes, it was recommended that an English teacher not be responsible for more than 100 students.

Diversified programs for the development of skills marketable by students who would terminate full-time education upon graduation from high school were advocated by Conant. He suggested that programs should be available for all girls who were interested in developing skills in typing, stenography, the use of clerical machines, and home economics. He proposed development of distributive education programs and, in rural areas, vocational agriculture, as well as trade and industrial programs depending on the community.

Conant advised communities to constantly reassess employment situations to determine what kinds of vocational programs are needed and to make them available. Students enrolled in these programs aimed at developing marketable skills were to take all the subjects required for their general education and were not to be isolated from students electing more academically-oriented programs.

Three of Conant's recommendations dealt with what the school should provide in the areas of foreign languages, science, and twelfth-grade social studies. Conant was convinced that mastery of a foreign language was not possible in less than three or four years of study and felt that two years did not provide any real working knowledge of a language. Consequently, he recommended that a student who demonstrated ability in handling foreign languages be counselled to complete a four-year sequence in one such language.

On the other hand, a student who had real difficulty in foreign language should be counselled against continuing beyond the first year. By "mastery," Conant meant ability to read the literature and to converse with fluency and accuracy with a native-speaker of the language. His discussion of the details for this recommendation was one of the longest of any of his proposals.

With respect to science courses, Conant was very specific: all students should have a course in biology or physical science, with each course given in at least three ability-grouped sections. The prerequisites and standards are detailed for each section. At the twelfth grade, Conant proposed two physics courses—one requiring mathematics as a prerequisite and the other designated as "practical physics."

A twelfth-grade course on American problems or American government was to be required of all students, with each class grouped heterogeneously. Teachers were to encourage free discussion and controversial issues were to be examined. The purpose of the course was to "contribute a great deal to the development of future citizens of our democracy who will be intelligent voters, stand firm under trying national conditions, and not be beguiled by the oratory of those who appeal to special interests."[36]

This recommendation was related to Conant's suggestions for using the homeroom as the base for developing mutual respect and understanding between students differing in abilities and vocational interests. Homerooms were to be kept intact, insofar as possible, for the entire high school period of three or four years and were to be linked to an active, effective student council. Administrators were to persuade teachers to view their homeroom responsibilities as very important.

Conant included a number of suggestions dealing with the academically talented (top 15 percent) and the gifted (top 3 percent) students. With respect to the academically talented, in addition to the four years of English and three years of social studies required for all students (and to be offered in ungrouped sections), they were to take as a minimum four years of mathematics, three years of science, and four years of one foreign language. These 18 courses were to require at least 15 hours of homework weekly. A second foreign language or an additional course in social studies could be elected and the academically talented were to be encouraged to take a course which had no homework, such as art and music.

The academically talented were to be identified as early as possible so that they could be scheduled for 20 or more courses with homework during the four years of high school. The next lower 10-20 percent were "to be guided into similar but less rigorous programs."

36. *Ibid.*, pp. 75-76.

Each year, the principal was to prepare an "academic inventory," summarizing the programs of the twelfth grade, academically talented students to determine the proportion actually taking the courses recommended for the more able students. The percentage of academically talented students who went on to two- and four-year colleges was also to be determined. Conant suggested that this inventory might be published each year so that the implementation of the policy for the academically talented could be determined.

For the highly gifted students, Conant recommended special arrangements with a special guidance officer serving as a tutor for the group to see that they are challenged by course work and provided with opportunities to develop their special interests. Conant advocated that gifted students in the twelfth grade take one or more Advanced Placement Program courses. In his view, such courses could have a good influence on students of lesser ability by raising the tone of the entire academic program.

Advanced courses were to enroll only those students who had demonstrated by a grade of *C* or better that they have the ability to handle more advanced work. In all courses assumed to be sequential (e.g., mathematics, foreign languages, and science), demonstrated ability was to be required.

An academic honors list was to be published at the end of each marking period, such a list to include the names of students who had elected the courses recommended for the academically talented and had earned an average grade of *B*. Students who elected meaningful nonacademic sequences and whose achievement was outstanding would receive some sort of separate special recognition as an incentive.

Conant recommended that students not be given a rank-in-class based on their grades in all subjects. His feeling was that such ranking resulted in bright students electing easier courses to obtain higher grades and that rank-in-class was often misleading.

All students should have access to a developmental reading program, available on a voluntary basis. Conant recommended that schools have the equipment available and that teachers and counselors should encourage students to take advantage of a program designed to increase their reading speed and comprehension.

Conant gave special attention to what he called the "very slow readers," ninth grade students who read at a level of sixth grade or below. He suggested that such slow readers be given instruction in

English and social studies by teachers particularly sympathetic to the needs of such students and familiar with remedial reading techniques and special textbook materials. Conant would have the elective work of such students directed toward simple vocational work, not permitting them into regular vocational, distributive education, or commercial programs. Conant differentiated between slow readers and mentally retarded students and noted that the latter represented a special problem requiring special instruction.

Although he recognized that the topic of ability grouping was highly controversial, Conant recommended that in those subjects required for all students and for those electives drawing students with a wide range of ability, the students should be grouped according to their ability on a subject-by-subject basis. He was opposed to any across-the-board tracking of students—i.e., placing a student in a particular section in all courses.

Conant recommended that a seven- or eight-period school day be organized with the periods as short as 45 minutes each. The flexibility of the seven- or eight-period day was necessary in order to make possible electives in addition to the required courses. This was particularly essential if the academically talented were to be able to elect the wide academic program recommended.

In addition, Conant recommended that boards of education operate tuition-free summer school programs available to both the students who have to repeat a course as well as the bright and ambitious who would use the summer to broaden their scope of elective programs.

Not included as one of Conant's 21 recommendations, but a proposal which was to have considerable impact was his suggestion that the elimination of the small high school be "a top priority." He expressed the conviction that the elimination of the small high school (i.e., one with a graduating class of fewer than 100 students) was the number one problem in many states. Aside from this recommendation for a drastic reduction in the number of small schools, Conant saw no need for a radical alteration in the basic pattern of American education. It was through elimination of the small high school that more comprehensiveness was to be achieved.

In his memoirs, Conant commented on the reception of his report on *The American High School Today*:

> Those laymen who had been criticizing the public schools most vigorously (and to my mind unfairly) cried "Whitewash." Carr and

> my friends on the Educational Policies Commission, as well as most public school superintendents and high school principals, greeted the findings and recommendations with considerable enthusiasm. The parents liked the book. For several weeks it was high on the best-seller list, an unusual distinction in those days for a book about schools. The reception by the professors of education was not so cordial. Some felt the recommendations were too conservative, if not plain reactionary. Perhaps the fact that a layman (for that was my status in their eyes) had ventured to intrude into their field of evaluating and recommending curricula had aroused some hostility. But, by and large, the professional educators endorsed the report, taking exception to only one or two of the recommendations.[37]

Conant's assessment of the reaction to the report was pretty much on the mark. However, a number of criticisms were leveled at specifics in the report. There were those who asserted that Conant's previously expressed biases were simply restated and that he had found what he was looking for. Others felt that Conant was overly concerned with the academically talented and gifted and not sufficiently concerned with those for whom he recommended the acquisition of marketable skills.[38]

The academic inventory was designed for the academically talented only and the academic honor list seemed also to be aimed at this population. In contrast, Conant was seen as being far less specific in detailing the means for acquiring marketable skills, except for what were seen as stereotyped programs for boys and girls.

Conant was criticized for his concept of "general education" and his apparent equating the mandating of certain "required subjects" with a general education. For some, Conant's recommendations for general education did not differ from the conventional college-preparatory program. Also, there were those who argued that Conant seemed unaware of alternative curriculum patterns to the

---

37. Conant, *My Several Lives*, pp. 621-622.
38. In February, 1958, in the middle of Conant's study, the National Education Association convened some 200 educators and laymen for an invitational conference "to consider problems involved in finding and educating the academically talented pupil." James B. Conant served as chairman of the conference. The conference report includes both an introductory statement and the conference summary by Dr. Conant. Many of the suggestions regarding the academically talented are first stated in Conant's summary. See J. B. Conant, conference chairman, *The Identification and Education of the Academically Talented Student in the American Secondary School* (Washington, D. C.: National Education Association, 1958).

rigidly compartmentalized subjects and the Carnegie unit approach.

Some commentators compared Conant's recommendations with those of the 1893 report of the Committee of Ten,[39] which proposed four alternative programs and listed the subjects to be studied and the period of time for which each be studied. Unlike that report, however, Conant did not detail *what* was to be taught.

Other reactors were troubled by the notion that if students take courses with particular titles for a particular period of "years," they are assured of a quality educational experience. The content and processes within courses with similar titles varied considerably. When Conant was specific—such as advocating that half of the four-year period that English was studied should be devoted to composition and the writing of an average of a theme a week—some educators thought his recommendation too restrictive since it presumably disregarded other means of communication.

Some critics felt that Conant had given only lip service to the study of music and art by the academically talented, noting that while he urged that these subjects be elected, he also recommended that the academically talented choose a second foreign language and another course in social studies which would fill their already heavy course loads. Conant's suggestion that pupils spend an average of 10 to 15 hours a week in home study was questioned by those who saw homework as an obsolete notion in general and a problem to implement in many homes where conditions were generally unsatisfactory.

Conant's report served as the focus of considerable discussion and debate. Conant himself appeared before numerous groups. He was featured in a 16mm film which used two high schools, one in Oakland, California, and the other in Labette County, Kansas, to present the Conant study and to show what every secondary school should be equipped to provide for the varied interests and talents of all youth in a community. The film had wide circulation.

Numerous journal articles, speeches, and meetings dealt with the report. For example, a symposium "on problems of current interest in the social sciences and of particular interest to the citizens of Minnesota" was convened at the University of Minnesota. The report of that symposium noted:

---

39. Committee on Secondary School Studies, *Report of the Committee on Secondary School Studies* (Washington, D.C.: U.S. Government Printing Office, 1893).

The selection of the "Conant report" was not simply occasioned by its wide circulation and the interest thoughtful people had in its recommendations. The impressive degree of public interest evidenced in Dr. Conant's suggestions for strengthening American high schools recommended the "Conant report"; it was clear that there was a genuine concern with Dr. Conant's reflections on secondary education.[40]

John Gardner had written that there were those who said that the comprehensive high school could not provide good and appropriate education for all: "When a man like James Conant says it can be done, the nation must take notice."[41] The nation did indeed take notice.

## Continuing with America's Secondary Schools

JAMES B. CONANT IN 1959 DELIVERED the Inglis Lectures at Harvard University in which he examined what he called the "revolutionary transformation of the American high school" that had taken place between 1905 and 1930.

By 1930 the widely comprehensive high school was to be found in many sections of the country. Boys and girls were spending as much as half their time in grades eleven and twelve on courses designed to develop skills marketable on graduation; the art and music departments were expanding rapidly; Latin was disappearing from the curriculum except for a two-year course. Institutions of higher education, both private and public, were enrolling students whose only academic credential was a high school diploma, and by 1930 this often meant the graduate had a minimum exposure to those academic subjects considered essential twenty-five years before.[42]

Conant analyzed the history of the continuation schools—separate schools organized to provide for part-time students in response to the Commission on the Reorganization of Secondary

40. R. H. Beck *et al., Perspectives on the Conant Report* (Minneapolis: University of Minnesota, 1960), p. 1.
41. Conant, *The American High School Today,* p. x.
42. J. B. Conant, *The Revolutionary Transformation of the American High School* (Cambridge: Harvard University Press, 1959), p. 4.

Education's recommendation that education be organized so that every normal boy and girl would be encouraged to remain in school to the age of 18 on full-time if possible, otherwise on a part-time basis.[43] In 1919, New York had enacted a law which required employed youth ages 14-18 to attend continuation schools for at least four hours a week for 36 weeks a year. Every school district with a population of 5,000 or more was required to establish such a continuation school.

Conant traced the growth and sudden decline of such schools, some of which were to become separate full-time vocational high schools in New York City, and argued that the revolution did not occur because a "band of professors had decided, that for the future well-being of our society, it was essential that all American youth stay in school full time through grade twelve" and then "enlisted the teachers, as in a crusade, and persuaded state legislators to raise the age of compulsory attendance to force the boys and girls to stay in school"[44]

Instead, Conant believed that the short-lived experiment with continuation schools was a uniquely American approach to answer questions still with us:

> How can you satisfy the youth who have little academic ability and whose interests lie in the direction of getting a job and developing a manual skill? How can you at the same time provide a general academic education for this type of student through twelve grades (or at least eleven) and at the same time prevent boredom and frustration?[45]

Conant's view of the significance of the American high school—the comprehensive high school which won out over the separate continuation schools when the latter were essentially destroyed by the depression of the 1930s—was expressed as follows:

> If the free world survives the perils that now confront it, I believe historians in the year 2059 will regard the American experiment in democracy as a great and successful adventure of the human race. Furthermore, as an essential part of this adventure—indeed, as the basic element in the twentieth century—they will praise the radical

43. Commission on the Reorganization of Secondary Education, *Cardinal Principles of Secondary Education,* Bulletin 1918, No. 35 (Washington, D.C.: U.S. Government Printing Office, 1918).
44. Conant, *Revolutionary Transformation,* p. 5.
45. *Ibid.,* p. 23.

transformation of America's treatment of its children and of its youth. They will regard the American high school, as it was perfected by the end of the twentieth century, as not only one of the finest products of democracy, but as a continuing insurance for the preservation of the vitality of a society of free men.[46]

In *The Child, the Parent, and the State,*[47] Conant revised his Inglis Lectures plus three others he had given that year and invited the reader to imagine joining him on a visit to a high school which Conant had been to not long before. In this description, Conant painted a picture of what was his ideal comprehensive high school:

> It is located in a district of a medium-sized city where the rents are low and where, in periods of recession, the unemployment is high. The school is attended primarily by those who live in the district but also by a few who come some distance to enroll in certain vocational programs, which have a good reputation. Less than ten percent of those enrolled desire to enter a college on graduation, though more than one four-year institution is located in the city and offers free tuition. Not many more than this small fraction of the student body have the ability to handle satisfactorily the usual twelfth-grade course in physics, trigonometry or a foreign language. And the more able students (about ten percent) are, for the most part, enrolled in these courses.
>
> The vocational courses are well staffed and well supported and cover a wide range. A girl can go a long way toward becoming an expert in stenography, in office practice work, in running a beauty parlor, in catering and professional cooking; boys on graduation will have completed the equivalent of one year of apprentice work in auto mechanics, airplane mechanics, tool and die work, metal work, and similar trades. All the students, irrespective of their elective programs, are devoting half their time to the improvement of their skill in reading and writing, to the study of some mathematics and science, history, political science, the elements of economics, and to a discussion of current problems. Many, if not all, are benefiting from the courses in art and music and are learning something about the ways of a democracy by the operation of clubs and other extra-curricular activities. The vocational courses for a vast majority represent the vital core of the school program. They represent something related directly to the ambitions of the boys and girls and their parents.[48]

46. *Ibid.*, p. 29.
47. J. B. Conant, *The Child, the Parent, and the State* (Cambridge: Harvard University Press, 1959).
48. *Ibid.*, pp. 65-66.

Conant argued that only the collective action of local citizens in communities across the nation would bring about better high schools: "The responsibility for the sorely needed upgrading of our schools cannot be passed to the state legislature or to Congress. The responsibility rests on every citizen in the land."[49] Once again, he was writing for the interested citizens.

## Education in the Junior High School

IN WHAT HE TERMED HIS SECOND report to interested citizens, Conant wrote on a study he undertook in 1959-60 of the junior high school.[50] With his small staff, Conant visited 237 junior high schools in 90 school systems in 23 states. He based his comments on these visits as well as on what he heard from meetings with teachers and administrators.

Conant took note of the controversy regarding the organization of school systems and concluded that the placement of grades 7, 8, and 9 was less important than the program provided for adolescents. Nevertheless, he recognized a need for special competence by teachers in these grades and urged school boards to "do all in their power to maintain the status and prestige of the professional staff in grades 7 and 8 to create working conditions that will make teaching in these grades a satisfactory and rewarding experience."[51] His recommendations were aimed primarily at grades 7 and 8 since grade 9 had been assigned to high school in his first report.

As with his first report, *The American High School Today,* Conant sets forth his recommendations, again directed to boards of education responsible for the policy-making function of the school. The first recommendation sets out the subjects he would require for all pupils in grades 7 and 8: "English (including heavy emphasis on reading skills and composition), social studies (including emphasis on history and geography), mathematics (arithmetic except as

---

49. *Ibid.,* pp. 82-83.
50. J. B. Conant, *Education in the Junior High School Years* (Princeton: Educational Testing Service, 1960).
51. *Ibid.,* p. 13.

noted in Recommendation 2), and science."[52] (Recommendation 2 suggested that a small number of pupils should begin algebra in grade 8.)

Conant recommended that all students receive instruction in art, music, and physical education while boys were to take industrial arts and girls, home economics. Some, if not all, pupils were to have instruction in modern language on a conversational basis in grade 7. Essentially, the instructional program in grades 7 and 8 was to consist of required subjects, with electives not beginning until grade 9.

Conant urged that instruction in the basic skills of reading and arithmetic be continued "as long as pupils can gain from the instruction." Pupils of average ability were to read at or above grade level; those more able were to read considerably above grade level; and, by grade 9, even the poorest readers were to be at least at the sixth grade level.

Recognizing the controversy concerning block-time teaching and departmentalization, Conant proposed that in grade 7, a teacher have pupils for two or more periods for English and social studies. Other than this block, he advocated departmentalization in grades 7, 8, and 9.

Conant recommended that "instruction should be organized to provide intellectual challenge for the whole range of abilities found in school" and again suggested ability grouping on a subject-by-subject basis. He suggested a seven-period day or the equivalent in order to provide sufficient flexibility in scheduling so that students would not need to make choices between subjects such as science and foreign languages. In the ninth grade, the curriculum should provide for continuation of the required general education courses as well as some choice of electives as discussed in the high school report.

Meaningful homework was to be assigned in all three grades and teachers were to coordinate homework assignments in different subject areas. Conant advocated that high standards be maintained in the academic courses and cautioned that since some students took longer than others to develop academic skills "standards of accomplishment, not effort alone, are needed below the senior high school level in required courses."[53]

---

52. *Ibid.*, p. 16.
53. *Ibid.*, p. 28.

A rich extracurricular program—including such group activities as music and drama, assembly and homeroom programs, interest clubs, intramural athletics, and student council—should be provided. Conant believed that seventh and eighth graders were at an age "when a certain amount of self-government through the homeroom organization and a student council begins to have meaning in the development of an understanding of democracy."[54]

And at the high school level, Conant recommended a full-time specialist, or the equivalent, in guidance and testing for every 250-300 pupils in grades 7 and 8. He urged that boards of education provide certain minimum special facilities including a library stocked at the level recommended by the American Library Association, a gymnasium with locker rooms and showers, specially equipped home economics and industrial arts rooms, an auditorium or assembly space, and adequate cafeteria space.

Articulation between grade levels was seen as a serious problem and Conant urged coordination in each subject area on a K-12 basis. He proposed a balanced staff of 50 professionals for 1,000 pupils as the minimum acceptable ratio. Except for physical education instructors, teachers were to have a five-period teaching load involving 125-150 pupils per day. Physical education teachers could carry 200 a day, Conant thought. He suggested that duties peripheral to the main task of teaching be minimized or eliminated.

Finally, in Conant's view, "the difference between a good school and a poor school is often the difference between a good and a poor principal."[55] The principal was to be given the kind of assistance, e.g., assistant principals and clerical help, that would enable him to fulfill his leadership role.

A minimum of 125 pupils in each of grades 7 and 8 was required, Conant believed, in order to provide an effective junior high program. He asserted that no costly reorganization was needed as long as this minimum of 125 pupils per grade was reached.

Again, Conant observed that these recommendations, as were those in his first report, were "purposely conservative" representing established practice in a number of schools. He agreed that there were many new and interesting developments that might revolutionize instruction in the future but, until these met the test of time,

54. *Ibid.*, p. 22.
55. *Ibid.*, p. 37.

he saw "no inconsistency in adapting the best of current practices and looking forward to new ideas."[56]

The report on the junior high school seemed to evoke much less debate and discussion than did the report on the high school. T. H. Briggs reviewed the report and thought it deserved high praise. Because it was addressed to school board members and other interested citizens, Briggs thought the report would "arouse more lay interest of a practical rather than a sentimental kind and stimulate concerted action to bring about improvements that are obviously needed." Briggs concluded: "For his devoted work the entire public owes Dr. Conant a large debt of gratitude."[57]

## Slums and Suburbs: Schools in Metropolitan Areas

DURING HIS STUDY OF *Education in the Junior High School Years,* Conant made observations on schools in the metropolitan areas—city and slums and wealthy suburbs. After his visits, Conant believed that a lesson to be drawn "*is that to a considerable degree what a school should do and can do is determined by the status and ambitions of the families served.*"[58]

Although the neighborhoods in the large cities Conant visited contained various minority groups, his study focused primarily on "Negro slums," neighborhoods which were *de facto* segregated. Conant's examination of the social and familial conditions of these inner-city areas and the special educational problems found in the schools which served them caused him considerable concern. In his concluding observations, he wrote that "social dynamite is building up in our large cities in the form of unemployed out-of-school youth, especially in the Negro slums."[59]

56. *Ibid.*, p. 45.
57. T. H. Briggs, "The Conant Report on Junior High Schools," *NASSP Bulletin,* November 1960, p. 20.
58. J. B. Conant, *Slums and Suburbs: A Commentary on Schools in Metropolitan Areas* (New York: McGraw-Hill, 1961), p. 1.
59. *Ibid.*, p. 146.

The major problem in wealthy suburban schools, Conant thought, was "to guide the parent whose college ambitions outrun his child's abilities toward a realistic picture of the kind of college his child is suited for."[60] Conant recommended that expert guidance begin early to educate both the child and his parents regarding "the realities of college admission."

The California pattern of higher education—a three-tier system which includes two-year junior colleges—was one Conant thought should be examined by citizens. The prestige colleges should be viewed as essential for the very bright students who would eventually go on to graduate school for advanced degrees in the professions. Conant argued that the place to begin to set standards in American education of the more able students is in both secondary schools and college.

In the wealthy suburban schools, he urged encouragement of bright students to elect a program with five, rather than the traditional four academic subjects, as required in a school like New York's Bronx High School of Science. All such suburban schools, he thought, should be participating in the Advanced Placement Program.[61]

In the large city slums, on the other hand, he advocated more money, observing that the differential in expenditures between slums and suburbs "challenged the concept of equality of opportunity in American public education." Conant proposed that large city schools be given responsibility for educational and vocational guidance of youth until age 21, even after they have left school. In both the slums and suburbs, more attention was needed for developing meaningful courses for students with less than average abilities, expanding work-study programs for slow students, and providing at least auto mechanics for boys in large city high schools.

Conant was convinced that "the answer to improving Negro education in the large Northern cities is to spend more money and to upgrade Negro schools, many of which are in the slum, rather than to effect token integration by transporting pupils across attendance lines."[62]

Such *de facto* segregated schools should and could have fully integrated teaching staffs, however. Conant recommended more

60. *Ibid.*, p. 144.
61. *Ibid.*, p. 145.
62. *Ibid.*, p. 146.

teachers and even more pay for teachers in the slums than for those in the wealthier districts of the large cities or the suburbs and suggested special training programs for such teachers.

In his report, Conant deliberately "sought to create a set of anxious thoughts in the minds of the conscientious citizens" who read his book, including those who worked in the cities but lived in the suburbs. As many came to realize later, Conant saw inner-city schools improving only as the lives of the families from which the students came improved. And, without a radical change in the employment of black youth, he saw little being accomplished.

Conant closed his report by urging more detailed analysis of urban educational problems so that the American people would better understand the dangerous social situation which existed. He was to be proved right about the social dynamite of our inner cities.

As he noted in his memoirs, reactions to *Slums and Suburbs* were quite mixed. Conant was particularly disappointed in the reactions of most of the outstanding black educational leaders who acknowledged his service in awakening the public conscience but found his position unacceptable. His recommendation that more money be spent on improving and upgrading black schools rather than busing pupils across attendance lines was viewed by black leaders as a return to the "separate but equal doctrine" at a time when they were striving for desegregation.

Conant observed that, in retrospect, he probably should have sought an alliance, made peace with the black leaders, and issued a second clarifying statement. But, as he put it, "I decided that, rightly or wrongly, I had become *persona non grata* for those who were in the midst of the problems of the urban schools. I turned my attention to another field—the education of teachers."[63]

## The Education of American Teachers

AT AN EARLY MEETING AT WHICH Conant was preparing a two-year study of the process of recruiting and training teachers, William Carr, the National Education Association's executive secretary, warned him that no matter what he reported, the reaction that

63. Conant, *My Several Lives*, p. 623.

would follow this report would make all the other attacks he had ever received seem like nothing in comparison.[64] Carr's prediction was to prove quite accurate.

Conant and his staff visited 72 institutions of all types in 22 states plus the state education departments in 16 states. As in the study of the high school, Conant visited classes and talked with students, teachers, and administrators. He estimated that he had talked to between 300 and 400 students in groups. His report [65] details his findings and sets forth no fewer than 27 recommendations.

Commenting on the report, Koerner, who had himself written a book titled *The Miseducation of Teachers*[66] several months earlier, predicted that Conant's image as a "mild and conciliatory inspector-general of education" would now be drastically changed:

> . . .for this time he is nothing less than insurrectionary. He proposes a sort of *coup d'etat* in the political structure of teacher education and a sweeping decentralization of power; he proposes the re-establishment of the institutional autonomy that has been so badly eroded over the last few decades; and he proposes to make academic excellence among the faculty and students of education the *sine qua non* of a good training program. All this, I submit, adds up to a revolution, or at least a proposed revolution.[67]

Conant's 27 recommendations dealt with every aspect of the recruitment and training of teachers, from the traditional quarrel between professors of education and professors of the academic subjects, to the locus of control of teacher training programs, to the accreditation and certification procedures, to inservice education, to the relations of state departments of education to teacher training institutions, and much more.

Conant proposed development of a position of "clinical professor," to be filled by individuals well grounded in both pedagogy and an academic discipline; teachers experienced at both the school and college level, who would teach methods, supervise student teachers, and play the same role in a school setting as the clinical

---

64. *Ibid.*, pp. 623-624.
65. J. B. Conant, *The Education of American Teachers* (New York: McGraw-Hill, 1963).
66. J. D. Koerner, *The Miseducation of Teachers* (New York: Houghton-Mifflin, 1963).
67. ________, "Proposals for Radical Reform," *Phi Delta Kappan*, October 1963, p. 7.

professor does for medical students at a teaching hospital. He also recommended greater use of examinations at frequent points to determine student competence—such examinations to replace reliance on courses and credits. Conant proposed that supervised student teaching become crucial in the certification process. The stress in teacher education, as Conant saw it, was to be on competence and such competence was to be judged by performance and not by credits alone.

Conant advocated recruiting potential teachers only from the top 30 percent of the high school graduates and providing a broad academic or general education during their first two years at college. Conant would replace certification based on courses and credits with a license based on *"how the teacher actually performs in a classroom."* Conant questioned both the necessity and the wisdom of a mandatory fifth year of training, especially if his proposals for the baccalaureate degree were implemented. Conant would have school boards give up their practice of giving raises on the basis of additional graduate courses in education and would instead provide increments only on the attainment of a graduate degree in an academic discipline.

With respect to the particularly thorny issue of accreditation of teacher training programs, Conant's recommendation was that the National Council for Accreditation of Teacher Education (NCATE) be made an "advisory" agency. Some of the sharpest debates set off by his recommendations centered on the need for and approach to national accreditation.

Sharply critical of many education courses—particularly the so-called "foundations of education" courses—Conant recommended strengthening such work by having those courses taught by well-trained academicians who evidenced a "commitment to public schools and their improvement." He thought general methods courses had little or no value and proposed specific methods be taught by the clinical professors who would be able to integrate methods with practice teaching and with the evaluation of student teachers. Conant argued for all-institutional involvement in teacher preparation and a sharing of power by the professors of education and those in the liberal arts.

In Koerner's view, the adoption of only the first five of Conant's recommendations, those which dealt with the licensing and practice of teaching, would "shake the industry of teacher training to its roots." Were all or most of the other recommendations implemented on a national scale, it would, Koerner believed, "radically transform the largest segment of American higher education and would involve a sort of academic genocide among this generation of professional educators, very few of whom would be qualified to continue doing what they now do."[68]

*The Education of American Teachers* proved to be highly controversial because Conant had tackled head-on all aspects of the politics of teacher education. Lindley J. Stiles wrote of the response to the book as follows:

> Perhaps no recent book on education has enjoyed the initial reception accorded this one. Its sales exceeded 50,000 copies within three months, and it continues on many best-seller lists. It was chosen as a Book-of-the-Month Club alternate selection. Within a month after publication, radio and television networks had featured it, and newspapers and popular as well as professional journals, reportedly over 1,200, had rushed into print with extensive reviews.
>
> . . .lay organizations. . .are devoting meetings to teacher education. Professional associations are centering their attention on the criticisms and recommendations advanced. Members of Dr. Conant's staff, as well as other leaders in teacher education, find it difficult to keep up with invitations to speak to interested groups. . . . Unlike previous criticisms of teacher education that were ignored by the professionals and unread by the public, this book seems destined to get a hearing.[69]

Conant wrote that as he looked forward to the publication of the report, he saw considerable trouble ahead: "Without abandoning my interest in education, I needed a new project. I was soon to find it, thanks to the Mayor of Berlin and the Ford Foundation."[70] In September 1963 Conant went off as adviser to the new Pedagogical Center being developed in West Berlin. During the year, however, he did return to address groups, including the American Association of Colleges of Teacher Education, on his views of teacher education.

68. *Ibid.*, p. 9.
69. L. J. Stiles, "Dr. Conant and His Critics," *Teachers College Record*, May 1964, pp. 713-714.
70. Conant, *My Several Lives*, p. 624.

## Shaping Educational Policy

CONANT'S NEXT REPORT DEALT with the matter of determining educational policy in a country where education had become a national concern. There had been many changes affecting public education and, in Conant's view, there would "be more radical changes in the future and this in turn means that our old methods of determining educational policy need drastic revision to meet the impact of the educational revolutions."[71]

On the basis of his experiences with the high school, Conant pointed to the tremendous diversity found in a highly decentralized public school system which boasted of its flexibility, independence, and innovation. While he thought that to date the students had not paid too high a price for such diversity, he foresaw that in the not-too-distant future, "revolutionary changes in the school curricula, with increasing emphasis on sequential subjects—foreign languages and mathematics—will produce so much diversity that the public will demand that some order be restored by one method or another."[72]

The educational policy for the public schools has largely been determined by educators concerned directly with the schools and with teacher educators, Conant believed, with implementation by chief state school officers and superintendents of the larger districts. He was convinced "that any amorphous unofficial body composed of public school administrators and professors of education is not now well suited to establishing policy for our public schools."[73]

Conant listed 10 problems facing public schools and then pointed out why the educational establishment (among whom he counted himself) was not able to deal adequately with any of them on a policy level. A drastic alteration in the ways of shaping educational policy was needed.

The tenth problem of Conant's list, segregated schools, was examined in great detail in the context of the comprehensive high school. He noted that those who have written in support of the comprehensive high school as a school which responds to and is

71. J. B. Conant, *Shaping Educational Policy* (New York: McGraw-Hill, 1964), p. 4.
72. *Ibid.*, p. 6.
73. *Ibid.*, p. 8.

conditioned by all types of groups and social classes had clearly turned their backs on the obvious exception to that definition—the education of the Negro.

> A comprehensive high school is a school in which *all* of the youth of an area attend the same school, or so we have often said. . . . It has been attacked because youth with different abilities, interests, and ambitions are all enrolled in one and the same school; the claim has been made that the intellectually more able should attend separate academic high schools and those who want practical courses should attend vocational schools. . . . The comprehensive high school has been defended on social and political grounds as an instrument of democracy, a way of mitigating the social stratification of society. Such has always been my argument. But neither I nor anyone else, as far as I am aware, has underlined the fact that in the former Confederate States no comprehensive high schools have ever existed. . . . And I said not a word to indicate that certain schools I visited were comprehensive only insofar as white youth were concerned.[74]

It was clear to Conant that neither the establishment nor the state educational administrative hierarchy had faced up to the problem of segregated schools and that while educators alone could not possibly formulate policy with respect to this issue, they could certainly help. In his view: "State by state certain basic issues should be faced, state by state a policy should be hammered out, and lay opinion here would be far more important than the views of educators."[75]

After analyzing policy making in higher education and in the two most populous states, New York and California, Conant argued that the "jumble of influential private and public bodies does not correspond to the needs of the nation in the 1960s. Some degree of order needs to be brought out of the chaos, primarily for the benefit of the on-coming generations, but also, to achieve a more effective use of public and private moneys."[76] Some form of cooperative exploration of educational problems by the federal government and the states was absolutely imperative.

Conant's suggestion was specific:

> Let the fifty states, or at least fifteen to twenty of the more populous states, enter into a compact for the creation of an "Interstate Com-

74. *Ibid.*
75. *Ibid.*, p. 47.
76. *Ibid.*, p. 109.

mission for Planning a Nationwide Educational Policy." The compact would have to be drawn up by the states and approved by Congress. The document would provide for the membership of the commission and provide the guidelines for its operation. Each state would be represented, though a group of less populous states might decide to be represented by one person. Each state would be ready to listen to any conclusions of the commission, but of course, would not be bound to follow its recommendations.[77]

Conant made detailed proposals about how the commission might work and gave examples of some of the issues they could tackle. John Gardner reacted favorably to Conant's proposals, sent a copy of the book to Terry Sanford, the outgoing governor of North Carolina, who proceeded "in the next twelve months to turn a rather sketchy idea into a definite proposal backed by many governors, chief state school officers and not a few educators."[78]

The result was the establishment in 1966 of the Education Commission of the States. Conant ends his memoirs as follows:

> Today, from what I have heard, though the strengthening of the state departments of education has been progressing slowly, the prospects are bright for a useful role for the Education Commission of the States. I admit to a considerable degree of satisfaction. An inventor, like a writer, is not free from the pride of authorship.[79]

## The Second Report: The Comprehensive High School

THE SECOND STUDY OF THE comprehensive high school was financed by the National Association of Secondary School Principals. This second look at the American high school was "concerned primarily with the opportunities for studying a variety of subjects in 2,000 widely comprehensive schools of medium size"[80] and was carried out through the use of questionnaires. The results indicated con-

77. *Ibid.*, pp. 123-124.
78. Conant, *My Several Lives*, p. 648.
79. *Ibid.*, p. 649.
80. J. B. Conant, *The Comprehensive High School: A Second Report to Interested Citizens* (New York: McGraw-Hill, 1967).

siderable differences among schools and variations among the states.

Using the criteria developed for the first study, Conant concluded that only a few schools could be regarded as highly satisfactory. However, he felt that the situation regarding academic studies in many of the schools was far better than it had been 10 years earlier.

Conant was convinced that an excellent comprehensive high school could be developed in any school district providing the enrollment was at least 750 students and sufficient funds were available. However, he observed: "As one examines the returns from different schools and different states, it becomes apparent that the American ideal of equality of educational opportunity is far from being realized. What emerges is a challenge to each community and each state."[81] Conant hoped that the report would arouse an informed electorate to the need for both study and action.

Medium-sized was defined as having a student enrollment of between 750-1,999. Schools from which fewer than 25 percent or more than 75 percent went on to further education were eliminated. Conant found that within the limits he imposed, size seemed to make little difference except with respect to the school's ability to offer a wide program in foreign language and opportunities for advanced placement.

In Conant's mind, a minimum of five criteria had to be met for a widely comprehensive high school. These are:

1. Provide instruction in calculus;
2. Provide instruction in modern foreign language for four years;
3. Arrange the schedule so that a student may study in any one year English, mathematics, science, a foreign language, social studies, physical education, art or music;
4. Provide one or more advanced placement courses;
5. Have enough English teachers so that "the average pupil load" is 120 or less.[82]

On the basis of correlating staff-student ratios with each of these five criteria, Conant concluded: *"If one is seeking any one single criterion to use as the basis of a first approximation to a judgment as to the adequacy of the offerings of a medium-size widely comprehensive school, the certified professional staff-student ratio is to be*

81. *Ibid.*, p. 2.
82. *Ibid.*, p. 17.

*recommended.*"[83] But the tremendous variations in staff-student ratios caused Conant to question whether the public school system was providing equality of opportunity.

The questionnaire returns indicated that the recommendation that there be a full-time counselor for every 250-300 students was far from a reality (only 13.9 percent of the schools had a ratio of 1 to 299 or less). Recognizing that it was difficult to ascertain the content of courses through questionnaires (e.g., schools list journalism, public speaking, and drama as "English courses"), he did not attempt to determine whether his earlier recommendation regarding required subjects was being implemented. He did find that 99 percent of the schools offered instruction in music and 86 percent offered art so that students did presumably have access to those electives.

The controversy concerning ability grouping, Conant thought, had subsided somewhat since 96.5 percent of the principals indicated that they did group students by ability in one or more academic subjects. Almost 92 percent reported that classes were available for students of lower ability. While 80 percent of the schools reported that summer school programs were available, only 58 percent indicated that such programs provided enrichment for the bright and ambitious students as well as opportunities for making up work for others.

The basis of general education in the comprehensive high school, Conant had recommended, was to be four years of English and four years of social studies, including two years of history (one of which was to be American history) and a twelfth grade course in American government or American problems. Only 24.9 percent of the schools required four years of social studies, but another 43.4 percent required three years. Seventy-one percent required a course in problems of democracy with 62.5 percent organizing such classes with a cross-section of the student body. Only 25.5 percent of the schools reported that teachers of English had a student load of 119 or less as Conant had recommended.

The returns indicated that in a majority of schools, academically talented students could schedule seven subjects (English, science, mathematics, foreign language, social studies, physical education, and art or music). Advanced Placement Program courses, recommended for the highly gifted, were available in fewer than a third of

83. *Ibid.*, p. 18.

the schools, however. Conant was pleased to find that a majority of the schools agreed with his recommendation concerning study of a foreign language, with 64 percent having arranged to offer instruction for four years in at least one modern language. A radical change had taken place in the foreign language situation in many schools.

The survey found that 92.4 percent of all the schools listed a course in business education and 90 percent a course in home economics. However, these constituted a very limited "vocational" offering. Conant noted that "there are so many changes in the whole field of vocational education that it would be worse than useless for me to attempt a diagnosis, let alone a prognosis."[84] He reiterated his belief that vocational work should be available in the comprehensive high school rather than a separate vocational school—his reasons being largely social rather than educational. Conant was convinced "that one of the fundamental doctrines of American society is equality of status in all forms of honest labor as well as equality of opportunity."[85] The widely comprehensive high school could contribute to that goal.

Because the comprehensive high school had been criticized for not providing adequately for the brightest students, Conant had stressed the kinds of opportunities that he thought should be made available to them. He concluded that considerable progress had been made in the intervening 10 years in the teaching of mathematics, science, and foreign languages.

Concerning new technology, Conant foresaw exciting developments. He saw the classroom teacher having at his disposal the equivalent of a library of instructional material, including television, and envisaged the school library transformed into a center for learning resources. The survey revealed, however, that 40 percent of the schools still did not meet the American Library Association's minimum standards.

Conant thought that the time was not too distant when "it will be the rule for a state to envision the task of educational authorities as the planning of a fourteen-year course of study for all or almost all youth."[86] When that occurred, he believed that some of the present vocational courses might well be displaced to grades 13 and 14. In

84. *Ibid.*, p. 62.
85. *Ibid.*
86. *Ibid.*, p. 77.

addition, elective courses in mathematics and foreign languages could be recast in terms of grades 10 through 14.

The possibility of structural changes—redrafting of district lines and shifting of the financial basis for instruction in grades 9 to 14—should not be overlooked. However, Conant cautioned:

> Whatever alternatives may seem advisable in providing the best instruction, due weight must be given to the social factor that is so prominent in arguments in favor of the comprehensive high school. Today there can be no question that public schools should operate within an *elective* and not a *selective* framework.[87]

Conant concluded his second report to interested citizens with the hope that would move public education ahead toward greater equality of opportunity during the next decade.

> It is clear that a secondary school with a favorable staff-student ratio can provide effective guidance and rich programs suited to students with diverse interests and varying abilities. Once the significance of well-supported comprehensive high schools is fully grasped, I believe support will be forthcoming. *Under such conditions these characteristic institutions may well prove to be the most powerful instruments for the rapid improvement of the education of all the nation's youth.* (Emphasis added)[88]

James Bryant Conant's commitment to the comprehensive public high school and its potential as a force in nurturing democracy in America had not waivered.

## Secondary Education One and Two Decades Later

TWENTY YEARS AFTER JAMES B. CONANT began his study of the American high school and 10 years after he published his second report on the comprehensive high school, American secondary education continues to be the focus of almost continuous study and criticism.[89]

87. *Ibid.*, p. 78.
88. *Ibid.*, p. 80.
89. For an analysis, see A. H. Passow, *Secondary Education Reform: Retrospect and Prospect* (New York: Teachers College, Columbia University, 1976).

Beginning in 1972, a number of committees, commissions, and panels have been examining the education and socialization of American youth.

A Kettering Foundation-supported National Commission on the Reform of Secondary Education was given a charge to "make a comprehensive examination of secondary education and provide the American public with a clear, factual picture of their secondary schools, indicating where and how they can be altered to better serve the nation's young people."[90]

A United States Office of Education National Panel on High School and Adolescent Education was given the task of preparing a report:

> . . .that would describe the current status of secondary education in the United States; identify and analyze the problems of adolescent education in American society today; ascertain the kinds of reform, renewal, and change needed, if any; and provide a description of the policy issues, and research and development programs that would make available needed knowledge and perspective.[91]

A Panel on Youth of the President's Science Advisory Committee had as its purposes:

> . . .to examine the contexts that now exist for youth, within which they come to adulthood, and assess the fitness of those contexts for the accomplishment of the developments necessary to full maturity, and then to propose alternative settings that seem to be preferable ways of accomplishing that assignment.[92]

The National Association of Secondary School Principals in 1974 appointed a task force to "examine the nature of modern youth, the contemporary social scene, and the place of secondary education within that scene."[93] Two years earlier NASSP's National Committee on Secondary Education conducted an invitational conference

90. B. F. Brown, chairman, The National Commission on the Reform of Secondary Education, *The Reform of Secondary Education: A Report to the Public and the Profession* (New York: McGraw-Hill, 1973), p. xiv.
91. J. H. Martin, chairman, National Panel on High School and Adolescent Education, *The Education of Adolescents* (Washington, D.C.: U.S. Government Printing Office, 1976), p. vii.
92. J. S. Coleman, chairman, Panel on Youth of the President's Science Advisory Committee, *Youth: Transition to Adulthood* (Chicago: University of Chicago Press, 1974).
93. National Association of Secondary School Principals, *Secondary Schools in a Changing Society: This We Believe,* (Reston, Va.: NASSP, 1975), p. vii.

to examine the prospects of experiential learning (or action learning, as the committee called it) and to share ideas on how best to broaden options and establish action-learning opportunities for young people in the 15 to 20 age bracket.

There were other reports of "studies" and conferences, each one setting forth the symptoms of serious dissatisfaction with the high schools of today. Each attempts to diagnose the nature and causes of the problems they identify. Each has recommendations for policy and program changes.

All of the studies done in the first half of the 1970s followed a very turbulent period in the late 1960s. By 1970, for example, it was reported that serious student disruptions had occurred in more than two-thirds of all urban and suburban schools and in more than half the rural high schools. Their criticisms of the school focused on many of the same aspects that Conant had attended to earlier but, in many areas, their recommendations differ drastically.

The Kettering Commission described the American high school as a "stormy petrel" whose existence "has always been controversial and often turbulent." A report of a conference sponsored by the Educational Facilities Laboratories (EFL) spoke of "the ailing condition of that unloved and troubled institution" which had caused a critic to describe the high school as "the most absurd part of an educational system pervaded by absurdity."[94] The USOE Panel on High Schools and Adolescent Education argued that "in attempting to meet the needs of all American youth, the high school today is often failing to respond adequately to the needs of individual students."[95]

The USOE Panel observed that there were "major problems in the secondary schools and in adolescent growth and development—manifest unrest and frequent racial conflict, a growing drug problem, inadequate preparation for work or for higher education, alienation and lack of motivation" and little effort was "being made to analyze these problems, their causes, and approaches to solutions."[96]

As Passow put it:

> Current criticisms of secondary education, the bases for reform

94. R. Weinstock, *The Greening of the High School* (New York: Educational Facilities Laboratories, 1973), p. 8.
95. *The Education of Adolescents,* p. 10.
96. *Ibid.,* p. vii.

proposals, range far and wide—from a questioning of the basic objectives of youth education, to misgivings as to whether a single institution such as the high school can provide "a complete environment giving all the necessary opportunities for becoming an adult," to concerns about the nature and relevance of curriculum, to apprehension about violence and vandalism preventing schools from functioning at all, to reconsideration of the roles and the exercise of power among various groups involved in educating youth.[97]

The USOE Panel recommended: *"That the unattained practice and inadequate concept of the comprehensive high school be replaced with the more practical goal of providing comprehensive education through a variety of means including the schools."* The Panel decided that the concept of the comprehensive high school had imposed on that one institution "all the variations in programs and services required to serve the needs of an extraordinarily diverse population." The result, they felt, was "oversized institutions, increasingly difficult to manage, artificially held to narrow pedagogic practices, overburdened with custodial responsibility and isolated from the community."[98]

The Panel on Youth of the President's Science Advisory Committee included, among its recommendations for creating new environments for youth education, a change in school structure that would include the "development of genuine specialization among high schools including but not limited to academic specialties" with free choice by youth among these specialized high schools.[99]

Moreover, the Panel on Youth proposed that the new specialized high schools should probably have not more than 500 students in them. The Panel on Youth recognized that these proposals went directly counter to the trends in American education toward comprehensive schools and for larger schools. The USOE Panel also argued for smaller high schools:

> Despite the assumption behind Conant's call for larger schools linking curricular diversity to the teacher-pupil ratio and the classroom setting, the Panel feels that the development of different instructional modalities, varying pupil-teacher ratios from tutorial and seminar situations to large groups has removed the requirement for school size to reduce cost. The Panel questions the assumption that

97. Passow, *Secondary Education Reform*, pp. 3-4.
98. *The Education of Adolescents*, p. 10.
99. *Youth: Transition to Adulthood*, pp. 152-153.

bigness *per se* is necessary for curricular diversity and feels that the desired diversity can be achieved in numerous other ways.[100]

The USOE Panel concluded that the concept of the comprehensive high school not only has not solved all the problems of adolescent education but has, in fact, increased them. The Panel observed that three benefits had been anticipated—financial, educational, and social. But, the Panel argued that "unfortunately, increasing evidence indicates that the large, comprehensive school has not been naturally money-saving, educationally advantageous, or broadly socializing and egalitarian."[101]

In the view of the USOE Panel, the large comprehensive high school "has failed to provide true breadth of courses, either because comprehensiveness is applied in only one area (college prep) or because the courses which supposedly offered to broaden student options really attracted only students with a negative self-image."[102]

The issues of general education and of curriculum in general are not examined by these reform groups in the same way as Conant did when he recommended required subjects as part of general education or when he proposed specific subjects and programs for the academically talented and the highly gifted. The USOE Panel suggested that a comprehensive education for adolescents must provide an appropriate balance and curriculum mix in five domains: personal values, citizenship, the arts, the humanities, and career education.

The panel, however, did not discuss specific subjects. It did propose educational programs involving both adolescents and adults in what they termed Participatory Education—"learning by doing what is socially useful, personally satisfying, and health-supporting for the individual and the community"—in the areas of education in arts, vocational education, and education in the operations of government for citizenship.[103]

Toward these ends, the panel recommended the creation of a community arts center closely associated with the high school, creation of a community career education center to provide a vehicle

100. *The Education of Adolescents,* p. 31. See also J. P. Sher and R. B. Tompkins, "The Myths of School Consolidation," *Educational Forum,* November 1976, pp. 95-107, also January 1977, pp. 137-153.
101. *Ibid.,* p. 25.
102. *Ibid.,* p. 26.
103. *Ibid.,* p. 10.

for new forms of vocational education, and involvement of adolescents with all appropriate governmental agencies to prepare them for citizenship.

The NASSP Task Force, recognizing certain sharp public differences on the purposes of secondary education, proposed that school site councils of parents, students, teachers, and administrators be formed to find a common ground for school action.

The task force also recommended that the curriculum be redesigned and placed in a more comprehensive setting. Opportunities for service and work, serious contact with adult institutions, and instruction in a variety of settings both on and off campus, NASSP believes, will broaden the definition of education beyond that commonly applied today.

Toward this end the principals recommended that schools assume the role of planner and broker for youth by "diagnosing the learning needs and styles" of students and by "locating and managing the total resource pool available to serve those needs" on the campus and in the community.[104] Also recommended were minimum competency tests in the basic skills for graduation and attention to values education.

The Kettering Commission recommended that all secondary school students, college preparatory or non-college bound, should receive a basic global education which would be "concerned with scientific, ecological, and economic issues which affect everyone." The Kettering Commission advocated a "basic international literacy" which would include enough history, politics, economics, and anthropology to provide students with "a sense of climate and natural resources and the trade routes that result."[105]

The Kettering Commission was also concerned with the decline in foreign language study which the committee viewed as contributing to an education in global affairs. The collapse of foreign language study, in the view of the Kettering Commission, strengthened the argument for a systematic program of global education. The commission would also alter most "Problems of Democracy" courses to focus on the impact of the world on the United States and vice versa rather than the variety of social issues now dealt with in most such courses.

---

104. *This We Believe*, p. 24.
105. *The Reform of Secondary Education*, p. 65.

While Conant had recommended electives from a somewhat restricted variety of academic and vocational subjects, most of the reports put emphasis on providing educational options and alternative programs. The Kettering Commission Task Force '74 categorized alternatives under two broad headings: one which deals with degree of structure, including the use of space and allocation of time; the second, including curricular design and the student population served.[106] The earlier Kettering Commission had recommended that the variety of options and alternatives open to students should be "limited by the legitimate needs of adolescents and the vivacity of the imagination of educational planners."[107]

Urging extension of the kinds of non-formal educational opportunities, the reports urge that schools reconsider their obsession with credentialling and accreditation and recognize that "authentic learning can take place in a wide variety of settings, many of them remote from the schoolhouse."[108]

The USOE Panel also urged consideration of "a wide selection of experience-based learning opportunities and programs in a given community," which the panel thought would be much "more capable of providing diverse learnings for the varied adolescent population than one or two conventional high schools."[109] The panel was sensitive to the possibility of the expansion of student and parent choices leading to segregation by increasing the likelihood of students choosing to be with others like themselves but felt that the school "should attempt to make each of its alternative institutions or learning opportunities as integrated (in terms of ethnic background, social class, age, etc.) as possible and should prevent such factors from being used as the basis for admission or exclusion."[110] In the USOE Panel's view, the comprehensive high school never really integrated youth from different backgrounds either.

Conant was concerned with the development of marketable skills and the improvement of vocational education, and many of the more recent reports focus on education for work and recommend the desigining of effective education-work policies. The USOE

106. J. W. Porter, chairman, Task Force '74, *The Adolescent, Other Citizens, and Their Schools* (New York: McGraw-Hill, 1975), p. xviii.
107. *The Reform of Secondary Education,* p. 101.
108. *Ibid.,* p. 75.
109. *The Education of Adolescents,* p. 57.
110. *Ibid.,* p. 57.

Panel, for example, proposed that youth be provided with real-jobs-with-real-work through a program that would emphasize job-knowledge, on-the-job training, occupational citizenship, and job placement.

The Kettering Commission recommended development of career education, realignment of curriculum "to provide students with a range of experiences and opportunities broad enough to permit them to take full advantage of career opportunities in their communities."[111] The Kettering Commission advocated career awareness programs, opportunities for exploration in a variety of career clusters, and opportunities to acquire hard skills in a career area but did not support the U.S. Office of Education concept of career education "that all educational experiences, curriculum, instruction, and counseling should be geared to preparation for economic independence and an appreciation for the dignity of work."[112]

The National Manpower Institute proposed "infusing the general education process with various forms of exposure to the meaning of work and service;" making actual work or service experience an integral part of all youth's education; and facilitating students' moving in and out of the educational and work sequence as seems appropriate for individuals.[113]

There are numerous other recommendations that appear in these reports urging reform of youth education and of the high school—such as lowering the compulsory attendance age, offering alternatives to the conventional 12-year schooling pattern, reducing the barriers to youth for work and service, arranging for furlough so that students can move in and out of school as appropriate and receive credit for experiences while on such a "considered break," providing for educational vouchers which can be used for a wide range of skill training as well as further education over a period of time, etc.

These reports point to a number of factors which now exist and should affect the design of education for adolescents—the end of the boom in education and declining enrollments due to zero-

111. *The Reform of Secondary Education,* p. 49.
112. *Ibid.,* p. 52.
113. W. Wirtz and the National Manpower Institute, *The Boundless Resource: A Prospectus for an Education/Work Policy* (Washington, D.C.: The New Republic Book Co., 1975).

growth population; the earlier physical and probably psychological maturing of adolescents; the increase in the diversity of high school populations; the impact of television, films and other mass media; the sharply altered socio-political climate; the ongoing struggle for control and governance of education; declining attendance; declining achievement; increase in vandalism and crime in the schools—to name just a few.

Thus, the panels, task forces, and commissions argue that times are changing, the context within which the schools operate have changed, the clienteles are different, but the American high school continues as it has for decades. The reports set forth recommendations for change of the entire delivery system of education of adolescents and youth, proposals which differ considerably from those Conant advanced 20 and 10 years ago. None of these reports has caught the interest of the wider public to the extent that Conant's "report to the interested citizen" did earlier.

Whether Conant would concur with the recommendations that have emerged from these new analyses and interpretations of the nature of youth and the socio-political settings in which they mature is impossible to determine, of course. His studies indicated that he was a shrewd, wise, and insightful observer who brought to the problems he was examining some very deep commitments to a set of ideas and ideals.

His championing of the comprehensive high school as a peculiarly American invention, constantly to be critiqued and improved in order to fulfill better its goal of serving *all* American youth, suggests that Conant would be sensitive to the new forces and the different conditions which affect this institution. If modifications and reform were needed for America to move forward in attaining equality of educational opportunity, to nuture social democracy, and to upgrade the experiences of our youth, one can be certain that James B. Conant would subject such proposals to the scrutiny of his sharp thinking.

In a review of *The American High School Today*, David Austin wrote:

> It is to be hoped that Dr. Conant's continuing study of other aspects of public education in the United States will provide even greater opportunities for the American public as a whole to sense the urgency of need for understanding the complex business of educating

young people for today and for the future. Certainly our schools have no greater champion in modern times than this distinguished gentleman and scholar.[114]

James Bryant Conant wrote for the interested citizen hoping to enlist his support in the improvement of educational opportunities for, as he always put it, *all* American youth.

---

114. D. B. Austin, "The Administrator and the Conant Report," *NASSP Bulletin*, May 1959, p. 202.

# Bibliography


Austin, David B. "The Administrator and the Conant Report," *NASSP Bulletin*, May 1959, pp. 193-202.

Beck, Robert H., *et al. Perspectives on the Conant Report.* Minneapolis: University of Minnesota, 1960.

Briggs, Thomas H. "The Conant Report on Junior High Schools," *NASSP Bulletin*, November 1960, pp. 13-20.

Brown, B. Frank, chairman, National Commission on the Reform of Secondary Education. *The Reform of Secondary Education: A Report to the Public and the Profession.* New York: McGraw-Hill, 1973.

Coleman, James S., chairman, Panel on Youth of the President's Science Advisory Committee. *Youth: Transition to Adulthood.* Chicago: University of Chicago Press, 1974.

Conant, James B. *Education and Liberty: The Role of the Schools in a Modern Democracy.* Cambridge: Harvard University Press, 1953.

________. *Education in a Divided World.* Cambridge: Harvard University Press, 1948.

________. *Education in the Junior High School Years.* Princeton: Educational Testing Service, 1960.

________. *My Several Lives: Memoirs of a Social Inventor.* New York: Harper and Row, 1970.

________. "Public Education and the Structure of American Society," *Teachers College Record*, December 1945, pp. 145-194.

________. *Shaping Educational Policy.* New York: McGraw-Hill, 1964.

________.*Slums and Suburbs: A Commentary on Schools in Metropolitan Areas.* New York: McGraw-Hill, 1961.

________. *The American High School Today: A First Report to Interested Citizens.* New York: McGraw-Hill, 1959.

________. *The Certification of Teachers: The Restricted State Approved Program Approach.* Washington, D. C.: American Association of Colleges for Teacher Education, 1964.

________. *The Child, the Parent, and the State.* Cambridge: Harvard University Press, 1959.

________. *The Citadel of Learning.* New Haven: Yale University Press, 1956.

________. *The Comprehensive High School.* New York: McGraw-Hill, 1967.

________. *The Education of American Teachers.* New York: McGraw-Hill, 1963.

________. *The Identification and Education of the Academically Talented.* Washington, D. C.: National Education Association, 1957.

________. *The Revolutionary Transformation of the American High School.* Cambridge: Harvard University Press, 1959.

________. *Thomas Jefferson and the Development of American Public Education.* Berkeley: University of California Press, 1962.

________. *Two Modes of Thought: My Encounters with Science and Education.* New York: Trident Press, 1964.

________. *Trial and Error in the Improvement of Education.* Washington, D. C.: National Education Association, 1961.

________ and Spaulding, F. *Education for a Classless Society.* Cambridge: Harvard University Press, 1940.

Cremin, Lawrence A. *The Transformation of the School: Progressivism in American Education,* 1876-1957. New York: Alfred A. Knopf, 1961.

Koerner, James D. *The Miseducation of Teachers.* New York: Houghton-Mifflin, 1963.

________. "Proposals for Radical Reform," *Phi Delta Kappan,* October 1963, pp. 7-10.

Martin, John H., chairman, The National Panel on High School and Adolescent Education. *The Education of Adolescents.* Washington, D. C.: U. S. Government Printing Office, 1976.

National Association of Secondary School Principals. *Secondary Schools in a Changing Society. This We Believe.* Reston, Va.: NASSP, 1975.

________. *Conference Report on American Youth in the Mid-Seventies.* Washington, D. C.: NASSP, 1972.

Passow, A. Harry. *Secondary Education Reform: Retrospect and Prospect.* New York: Teachers College Press, 1976.

Porter, John W., chairman, Task Force '74 . *The Adolescent, Other Citizens, and Their Schools.* New York: McGraw-Hill, 1975.

Sher, Jonathan P. and Tompkins, Rachel B. "The Myths of School Consolidation," *Educational Forum,* November 1976, pp. 95-107; also January 1977, pp. 137-153.

Stiles, Lindley J. "Dr. Conant and His Critics," *Teachers College Record,* May 1964, pp. 712-717.

Warner, W. Lloyd, Havighurst, Robert J., and Loeb, Martin B. *Who Shall Be Educated?* New York: Harper and Brothers, 1944.

Weinstock, Ruth. *The Greening of the High School.* New York: Educational Facilities Laboratories, 1973.

Wirtz, Willard, and the National Manpower Institute. *The Boundless Resource: A Prospectus for an Education/Work Policy.* Washington, D. C.: The New Republic Book Co., 1975.

# Appendix

# A. 21 Recommendations: *The American High School Today*

### Recommendation 1: The Counseling System

In a satisfactory school system the counseling should start in the elementary school, and there should be good articulation between the counseling in the junior and senior high schools if the pattern is 6-3-3 or between the counseling in the elementary school and the high school if the system is organized on an 8-4 basis. There should be one full-time counselor (or guidance officer) for every two hundred fifty to three hundred pupils in the high school. The counselors should have had experience as teachers but should be devoting virtually full time to the counseling work; they should be familiar with the use of tests and measurements of the aptitudes and achievement of pupils. The function of the counselor is not to supplant the parents but to supplement parental advice to a youngster. To this end, the counselor should be in close touch with the parent as well as the pupil. Through consultation, an attempt should be made each year to work out an elective program for the student which corresponds to the student's interest and ability as determined by tests of scholastic aptitude, the recorded achievement as measured by grades in courses, and by teachers' estimates. The counselors should be sympathetic to the elective programs which develop marketable skills; they should also understand the program for the slow readers and be ready to cooperate with the teachers of this group of students.

### Recommendation 2: Individualized Programs

It should be the policy of the school that every student has an individualized program; there would be no classification of students according to clearly defined and labeled programs or tracks such as "college-preparatory," "vocational," "commercial." In advising the student as to his elective program, the counselor will be guided by the minimum program recommended as a matter of school policy for the academically talented or by recommended sequences leading to the development of skills marketable on graduation. It will turn out that many students of similar ability and vocational interests will have almost identical programs, but a student who has elected an academic sequence may shift to a vocational sequence and vice versa. Furthermore, with individualized programs, the students themselves do not feel that they are labeled according to the program they have chosen in the ninth or tenth grade. If flexibility is combined with a declaration of policy in regard to the programs for the academically talented and if a good guidance service is available, the academic inventory should show results as satisfactory as the results in a school which has a clear-cut academic or college-preparatory track.

**Recommendation 3: Required Programs for All**

A. *General Education.* The requirements for graduation for all students should be as follows:

> four years of English, three or four years of social studies—including two years of history (one of which should be American history) and a senior course in American problems or American government—one year of mathematics in the ninth grade (algebra or general mathematics), and at least one year of science in the ninth or tenth grade, which might well be biology or general physical science. By a year, I mean that a course is given five periods a week throughout the academic year or an equivalent amount of time. This academic program of general education involves nine or ten courses with homework to be taken in four years and occupies more than half the time of most students, whatever their elective programs.

B. *The Elective Program.* The other requirement for graduation should be successful completion of at least seven more courses, not including physical education. *All students should be urged to include art and music in their elective programs.* All students should be advised to have as the central core of their elective programs significant sequences of courses, either those leading to the development of a marketable skill or those of an academic nature.

C. *Standards for Pass and Failure.* This recommendation is directed to the principal of the high school and involves the kind of policy with which a school board should not be directly concerned. In order to assist the counselors in their work of guiding the students into programs which the students can handle effectively, the teachers of the advanced academic *elective* courses—foreign languages, mathematics, and science—should be urged to maintain high standards. They should be told not to hesitate to fail a student who does not meet the minimum level of performance they judge necessary for a mastery of the subject in question. In other words, the work in the academic elective courses should be judged on a standard of performance so high that students who do not have the ability to handle the subjects are discouraged from electing these courses and prevented from continuing in the sequence. On the other hand, for the *required* courses another standard should be applied. Since these courses are required of all, irrespective of ability, a student may be given a passing grade if he has worked to full capacity whether or not a certain level of achievement has been reached. A series of examinations in English composition (Recommendation 6) should insure the development of a minimum skill in composition; an eleventh grade test in arithmetic followed by a remedial twelfth-grade course is likewise to be recommended.

**Recommendation 4: Ability Grouping**

In the required subjects and those elected by students with a wide range of ability, the students should be grouped according to ability, subject by subject. For example, in English, American history, ninth-grade algebra, biology, and physical science, there should be at least three types of classes—one for the more able in the subject, another for the large group whose ability is about average, and another for the very slow readers who should be handled by special teachers. The middle group might be divided into two or three sections according to the students' abilities in the subject in question. This type of grouping is not to be confused with across-the-board grouping according to which a given student is placed in a particular section in *all* courses, Under the scheme here recommended, for example, a student may be in the top section in English but the middle section in history or ninth-grade algebra.

**Recommendation 5: A Supplement to a High School Diploma**

The awarding of a diploma is evidence only that a student has (1) completed the required work in general education to the best of his ability, and (2) has finished satisfactorily a certain sequence of elective courses. In addition to the diploma, each student should be given a durable record of the courses studied in four years and the grades obtained. The existence of such a record should be well publicized so that employers ask for it rather than merely relying on a diploma when questioning an applicant for a job about his education. The record might be a card that could be carried in a wallet.

**Recommendation 6: English Composition**

The time devoted to English composition during the four years should occupy about half the total time devoted to the study of English. Each student should be required to write an average of one theme a week. Themes should be corrected by the teacher. In order that teachers of English have adequate time for handling these themes, no English teacher should be responsible for more than one hundred pupils.

To test the ability of each student in English composition, a schoolwide composition test should be given in every grade; in the ninth and eleventh grades, these composition tests should be graded not only by the teacher but by a committee of the entire school. Those students who do not obtain a grade on the eleventh-grade composition test commensurate with their ability as measured by an aptitude test should be required to take a special course in English composition in the twelfth grade.

## Recommendation 7: Diversified Programs for the Development of Marketable Skills

Programs should be available for girls interested in developing skills in typing, stenography, the use of clerical machines, home economics, or a specialized branch of home economics which through further work in college might lead to the profession of dietitian. Distributive education should be available if the retail shops in the community can be persuaded to provide suitable openings. If the community is rural, vocational agriculture should be included. For boys, depending on the community, trade and industrial programs should be available. Half a day is required in the eleventh and twelfth grades for this vocational work. In each specialized trade, there should be an advisory committee composed of representatives of management and labor. Federal money is available for these programs.

The school administration should constantly assess the employment situation in those trades included in the vocational programs. When opportunities for employment in a given trade no longer exist within the community, the training program in that field should be dropped. The administration should be ready to introduce new vocational programs as opportunities open in the community or area. In some communities, advanced programs of a technical nature should be developed; these programs often involve more mathematics than is usually required for the building trades or auto mechanics programs.

As stated in Recommendation 3 (a) the students enrolled in programs which develop marketable skills should also be enrolled in English, social studies, and other courses required for graduation. Furthermore, efforts should be made to prevent isolation from the other students. Homerooms may be effective means to this end (see Recommendation 20).

## Recommendation 8: Special Consideration for the Very Slow Readers

Those in the ninth grade of the school who read at a level of the sixth grade or below should be given special consideration. These pupils should be instructed in English and the required social studies by special teachers who are interested in working with such students and who are sympathetic to their problems. Remedial reading should be part of the work, and special types of textbooks should be provided. The elective programs of these pupils should be directed toward simple vocational work, and they should be kept out of the regular vocational programs for boys, the distributive education program, and the regular commercial program for girls. These students should not be confused with mentally retarded students. The education of the mentally retarded is a special problem which in some states is also handled in the regular high school through special instruction and the use of special state funds.

### Recommendation 9: The Programs of the Academically Talented

A policy in regard to the elective programs of academically talented boys and girls should be adopted by the school to serve as a guide to the counselors. In the type of school I am discussing the following program should be strongly recommended as a minimum:

Four years of mathematics, four years of one foreign language, three year of science, in addition to the required four years of English and three years of social studies; a total of eighteen courses with homework to be taken in four years. This program will require at least fifteen hours of homework each week.

Many academically talented pupils may wish to study a second foreign language or an additional course in social studies. Since such students are capable of handling twenty or more courses with homework, these additional academic courses may be added to the recommended minimum program. If the school is organized on a seven- or eight-period day (Recommendation 12), at least one additional course without homework (for example, art or music) may also be scheduled each year.

If as school policy a minimum academic program including both mathematics and a foreign language is recommended to the academically talented pupils and their parents, the counselors will have the problem of identifying as early as possible the members of the group. It may well be that, in the next lower 10 or 20 percent of the boys and girls in terms of scholastic aptitude on a national basis, there are a number who ought to be guided into similar but less rigorous programs.

### Recommendation 10: Highly Gifted Pupils

For the highly gifted pupils some type of special arrangement should be made. These pupils of high ability, who constitute on a national basis about 3 percent of the student population, may well be too few in number in some schools to warrant giving them instruction in a special class. In this case, a special guidance officer should be assigned to the group as a tutor and should keep in close touch with these students throughout their four years of senior high schoolwork. The tutor should see to it that these students are challenged not only by course work but by the development of their special interests as well. The identification of the highly gifted might well start in the seventh or eighth grade or earlier.

If enough students are available to provide a special class, these students should take in the twelfth grade one or more courses which are part of the Advanced Placement Program. This program has been developed in recent years by schools and colleges working cooperatively under the aegis of the College Entrance Examination Board. Under the program a student in the twelfth grade may take such courses as college mathematics, college English, or college history and, after passing suitable examinations, may be given college credit for the courses and also sophomore standing in these subjects. This program should be adopted not only because of the benefits which accrue to the students involved, but because it may well have a good influence on students of somewhat less ability by raising the tone of the whole academic program. Information about this program may be obtained by writing to the Director of the Advanced Placement Program, College Entrance Examination Board, 425 West 117th Street, New York 27, New York.

**Recommendation 11: The Academic Inventory**

In order to provide meaningful statistics about the education of the academically talented, a school board through the superintendent should ask the principal each year to provide an academic inventory. As explained earlier, the academic inventory summarizes the programs of the academically talented students in the senior class without giving their names. In a school in which the range of intellectual ability corresponds to the national norm, 15 percent of the students would be included in this inventory. In other schools the percentage may vary. The academic inventory should include information as to what per cent of the academically talented boys and girls went on to a two-year college, a four-year college, or a university. This academic inventory of the graduating class might well be published each year.

**Recommendation 12: Organization of the School Day**

The school day should be so organized that there are at least six periods in addition to the required physical education and driver education which in many states occupy at least a period each day. A seven- or eight-period day may be organized with periods as short as forty-five minutes. Under such an organization, laboratory periods as well as industrial arts courses should involve double periods.

The flexibility provided by such an arrangement is to be contrasted with the rigidity of that of the six-period day. With a six-period day, one period of which is taken up by physical education, the academically talented student cannot elect the wide academic program recommended above and at the same time elect art, music, and practical courses. The importance of this recommendation can hardly be over-emphasized in connection with the education of academically talented students.

**Recommendation 13: Prerequisites for Advanced Academic Courses**

Standards in advanced courses should be such that those who enroll in each successive course of a sequence have demonstrated the ability required to handle that course. To this end, admission to eleventh-grade mathematics should depend upon the student's receiving at least a *C* in tenth-grade mathematics, and for admission to twelfth-grade mathematics at least a *C* should be required in the eleventh-grade course. Similarly, if the physics course is given in the twelfth grade, it should be open only to those students who have studied three years of mathematics and obtained a grade of at least *C* in each course. Also, in the foreign language sequence, a grade of *C* should be required for entry into the second-year course.

### Recommendation 14: Students Should Not Be Given a Rank in Class According to Their Grades in All Subjects

In many schools, it is customary to designate a rank in class on graduation as determined by the marks received; the position of valedictorian is usually held by the student whose rank is number one. The ranking is calculated by averaging the grades in all subjects taken during the four years. I have found that in many schools the desire to rank high has led bright students to elect easy courses in order to obtain high grades. This fact emerges clearly from an examination of many programs sent to us by schools as part of their academic inventories. The use by some colleges and universities of rank in class as the basis of their admission policies has increased this tendency of bright boys and girls to avoid stiff programs. Following the practice in at least one school visited, I strongly recommend that the graduating class not be ranked on the basis of grades obtained in *all* subjects and that a valedictorian not be named on this basis. Admission officers in colleges and universities should be urged to examine the transcript of a student's entire record rather than to rely on the misleading rank in class.

### Recommendation 15: Academic Honors List

At the end of each marking period, a list should be published of the students who had elected courses recommended for the academically talented and had made an average grade of B. On graduation a notation might be made on the diploma if a student had placed on the academic honors list in all four years.

In order to provide an incentive for the election of a meaningful nonacademic sequence, those students whose achievement was outstanding in the courses that are usually labeled "commercial" or "vocational" should receive some special recognition. By such devices I believe the ambitions of students in various elective programs can be stimulated as much as by the granting of separate types of diploma.

### Recommendation 16: Developmental Reading Program

A school should have the equipment for a developmental reading program. The program should be available on a voluntary basis for all the pupils in the school. The counselors and teachers of English should be asked to view this program sympathetically and to urge students to take advantage of the opportunity to increase reading speed and comprehension.

**Recommendation 17: Summer School**

The school board should operate a tuition-free summer school in which courses are available not only for students who have to repeat a subject, but also for the bright and ambitious students who wish to use the summer to broaden the scope of their elective programs.

**Recommendation 18: Foreign Languages**

The school board should be ready to offer a third and fourth year of a foreign language, no matter how few students enroll. The guidance officers should urge the completion of a four-year sequence of *one* foreign language if the student demonstrates ability in handling foreign languages. On the other hand, students who have real difficulty handling the first year of a language should be advised against continuing with the subject (Recommendation 13). The main purpose of studying a foreign language is to obtain something approaching a mastery of that language. And by a mastery is surely meant the ability to read the literature published in the language and, in the case of a modern language, to converse with considerable fluency and accuracy with an inhabitant of the country in question.

**Recommendation 19: Science Courses**

All students should obtain some understanding of the nature of science and the scientific approach by a required course in physical science or biology. This course should be given in at least three sections grouped by ability (Recommendation 4).

To accommodate students who are interested in science but do not have the required mathematical ability, two types of chemistry courses should be offered. For entry into one, at least a *C* in algebra and tenth-grade mathematics should be required. The other course should be designed for pupils with less mathematical ability. The standards even in this second course, however, should be such that those with less than average ability (assuming a distribution of ability according to the national norm) will have difficulty passing the course.

In addition to the physics course given in the twelfth grade with mathematics as a prerequisite (Recommendation 13) another course in physics should be offered with some such designation as "practical physics." The standards in this second course should be such that students with less than average ability have difficulty passing the course.

**Recommendation 20: Homerooms**

For the purpose of developing an understanding between students of different levels of academic ability and vocational goals, homerooms should be organized in such a way as to make them significant social units in the school. To this end, students should be kept together in one homeroom for the entire senior high school course (three or four years), and care should be taken to have each homeroom a cross section of the school in terms of ability and vocational interest. The teachers in charge of the homerooms should be persuaded by the administration that their work as homeroom teachers is important. Sufficient time should be allotted to the homeroom so that students may use this period to develop a sense of community interest and to have practice in a small way in representative government. The homerooms should elect one or two representatives to the student council, and these representatives should report back after each meeting of the council. They should listen to the opinions of their constituents and be guided by their opinions in voting on matters before the student council. To be effective, the student council should be treated sympathetically by the school administrators so that there will be some important questions each year with which the student council can be concerned and which, in turn, can be presented to the homerooms by the representatives.

**Recommendation 21: Twelfth-Grade Social Studies**

In the twelfth grade a course on American problems or American government should be required. This course should include as much material on economics as the students can effectively handle at this point in their development. Each class in this course should be a cross section of the school: the class should be heterogeneously grouped. Teachers should encourage all students to participate in discussions. This course should develop not only an understanding of the American form of government and of the economic basis of our free society, but also mutual respect and understanding between different types of students. Current topics should be included; free discussion of controversial issues should be encouraged. This approach is one significant way in which our schools distinguish themselves from those in totalitarian nations. This course, as well as well-organized homerooms and certain student activities, can contribute a great deal to the development of future citizens of our democracy who will be intelligent voters, stand firm under trying national conditions, and not be beguiled by the oratory of those who appeal to special interests.

## B. 14 Recommendations: *Education in the Junior High School Years*

### Recommendation 1: Required Subjects for All Pupils in Grades 7 and 8

The following subjects should be required of all pupils in grades 7 and 8: English (including heavy emphasis on reading skills and composition), social studies (including emphasis on history and geography), mathematics (arithmetic except as noted in Recommendation 2), and science.

In addition, all pupils should receive instruction in art, music, and physical education. All girls should receive instruction in home economics and all boys instruction in industrial arts. (See Recommendation 10 for the program in grade 9.)

### Recommendation 2: New Developments in Mathematics and Foreign Languages

A small fraction of pupils should start algebra (or one of the new brands of mathematics) in grade 8. Some, if not all, pupils should start the study of a modern foreign language on a conversational basis with a bilingual teacher in grade 7.

### Recommendation 3: Basic Skills

Instruction in the basic skills begun in the elementary school should be continued as long as pupils can gain from the instruction. This statement applies particularly to reading and arithmetic.

Pupils with average ability should read at or above grade level; superior pupils considerably above grade level. By the end of grade 9 even the poorest readers (except the mentally retarded) should read at least at the sixth-grade level.

### Recommendation 4: Extra-Class Activities

Group activities which have particular relevance for early adolescents should be part of the total program. These include musical and dramatic activities, assembly and homeroom programs, interest clubs, intramural athletics, and student council.

### Recommendation 5: Block-Time and Departmentalization

Provisions should be made to assure a smooth transition for the young adolescent from the elementary school to the secondary school.

**Recommendation 6: Flexibility in Schedule**

The daily class schedule should be sufficiently flexible to avoid the necessity for pupils to make choices between, for example, science and foreign languages.

**Recommendation 7: Challenging All Pupils**

Instruction should be organized to provide intellectual challenge for the whole range of abilities found in a school.

**Recommendation 8: Guidance and Testing**

A full-time specialist, or the equivalent, in guidance and testing should be available for every 250-300 pupils in grades 7 and 8. The same ratio applies to grades 9-12 as well (See *The American High School Today*).

**Recommendation 9: Homework, Marking, and Promotion**

Meaningful homework is profitable in grades 7, 8, and 9; drudgery, however, is not meaningful homework. Teachers and principals should develop careful procedures to assure coordination of homework assignments between teachers of different subjects.

High standards should be maintained in academic courses in grades 7, 8, and 9 because of the necessity for mastery of basic skills. Some pupils take longer to develop these skills than other pupils, and this fact implies that standards of accomplishment, not effort alone, are needed below the senior high school level in required academic courses. This fact also implies that a few pupils might be held back, though certainly for no more than two years in the first eight grades.

**Recommendation 10: Program in Grade 9**

In the ninth grade, the curriculum should provide for the usual sequential elective program as well as the continuation of the required courses in general education. (See *The American High School Today*.)

**Recommendation 11: Minimum Special Facilities**

Satisfactory instruction requires that the following facilities be available for pupils in grades 7 and 8: (1) a well-stocked library (see *Standards for School Library Programs,* American Library Association, 1960); (2) a gymnasium with locker rooms and showers; (3) specially equipped home economics rooms for girls and industrial arts rooms for boys; (4) an auditorium or assembly space for at least half the student body; (5) cafeteria space for at least one-third of the student body.

**Recommendation 12: Coordination of Subject Matter Instruction**

Whatever the organization of a school system, there should be careful coordination in each one of the subject areas in grades K-12.

**Recommendation 13: Size of System-Wide Professional Staff and Teacher Load, Grades 7-12**

A balanced staff of 50 professionals for 1,000 pupils is the minimum acceptable ratio for an adequately staffed school system. A higher ratio of professional staff to pupils is desirable.

The teacher load in grades 7-12 should be approximately the same in most subject areas. The reasonable limits of this load are five teaching periods involving 125-150 pupils per day. Physical education teachers can carry a load of 200 pupils a day, whereas English teachers should be responsible for no more than 100 pupils. It is possible that a few teachers of advanced academic electives in the senior high school may also have somewhat smaller pupil loads. A professional librarian should be responsible for no more than 750 pupils.

Duties of teachers which are peripheral to the main task of teaching should be minimized and constantly re-evaluated. No other duty takes precedence over classroom instruction.

**Recommendation 14: Leadership Role of the Principal**

The difference between a good school and a poor school is often the difference between a good and a poor principal. A good school invariably means strong leadership by the principal. To exercise leadership, the principal must have sufficient administrative assistance in the form of assistant principals and clerical help. The extent of assistance should vary according to the size and nature of the school. Generally speaking, a full-time assistant principal at the secondary level should be available for every 750 pupils; a clerk or secretary should be available for every 250 pupils.

The question to be answered: Is the principal forced to spend a considerable fraction of his time doing routine tasks that could be done by either an assistant principal or secretary? If he is, he cannot perform his role as instructional leader; help should be provided.